Procter Brothers Publishers

Pleasure drives around Cape Ann

Procter Brothers Publishers
Pleasure drives around Cape Ann
ISBN/EAN: 9783337192907
Printed in Europe, USA, Canada, Australia, Japan
Cover: Foto ©ninafisch / pixelio.de

More available books at **www.hansebooks.com**

Pleasure Drives
Around Cape Ann

PROCTER BROTHERS, PUBLISHERS,
GLOUCESTER, MASS.

GLOUCESTER FROM EAST GLOUCESTER, SHOWING INNER HARBOR.

PREFACE.

THE drives about Gloucester prove most inviting and attractive, not only to our own people, but to the thousands of summer visitors who keenly enjoy them, for you find Nature so lavish with her charms, combining ocean, river, beaches, massive boulders, grand old woods with hill and dale, and producing such magnificent scenery, while its diverting variety furnishes hours of pleasure which are redolent with happy and delightful memories.

Just in the height of the season, when there are so many strangers in town, a few pen pictures of the most popular drives will serve to intensify the interest of tourists in Gloucester and introduce to them the places they should surely visit by carriage, and will lend color to their anticipations of the charms old Cape Ann can throw about them.

GLOUCESTER FROM CITY HALL TOWER (SOUTH), SHOWING OUTER HARBOR.

Drive to East Gloucester.

THE drive to this suburb of Gloucester gives one a most diversified and quaint view, for you skirt the harbor and pass through the business street of the city, eventually reaching one of the gayest, most charming and picturesque summer resorts on the North Shore.

The route gives views of the wharves, the principal business of this fishing city, which proves most interesting to the stranger, who can, if so disposed, turn aside from the regular road and spend a few leisure hours in gaining information relative to the catch and curing of fish. Don't be afraid to inquire, if you are the least interested, for our dealers always are glad to welcome such inquirers. Then again you may run across one of the old skippers who is done with salt water cruising and is working ashore, and you will find him ever ready to impart information and give an account of his experience, and live over again, as it were, in his vivid mind pictures, big trips, heroic deeds and other pleasing adventures.

Passing along Main Street a view of the principal business establishments, the banks, post office, etc., may be seen; then the ride through that vicinity known as the "Head of the Harbor," where many quaint buildings on high elevations attract the eye, and as you turn the bend of the road at the foot of Lufkin's Hill, a fine view of both inner and outer harbors is obtained.

Here we get a pretty marine picture of the fishing crafts and yachts lying at anchor or flitting over the harbor's surface, their white wings stretching out filled with the gentle breezes; also mammoth barks, ships or steamers from Trapani, Italy, or other foreign ports, at the wharves of John Pew & Son and Wm. Parsons, 2d & Co., or in the stream, discharging cargoes of salt, while the historic little island, "Five Pound," lying in the inner harbor, could, were it some centenarian, tell you of its significance during the Revolution.

After passing Lufkin's Hill we come upon the boat building factory of Messrs. Higgins & Gifford, notable for having built three dories which successfully crossed the Atlantic, one even crossing and recrossing safely, namely, Centennial, Nautilus and Little Western.

From this point also can be seen Fort Defiance, the peninsula of Rocky Neck, Ten Pound Island and Stage Fort. These points of interest with their surroundings are fitting attractions to one of the finest maritime pictures to be found on the New England coast. Ascending Point Hill it would be well to stop and view the prospect over, taking in the harbor scene again and the city, the Farms and their surroundings, and then drive slowly through the thriving suburb of East Gloucester.

Two churches, Methodist Episcopal and Baptist, situated within rifle shot of one another, give assurance that the spiritual wants of the people receive attention, while Independent Hall and the attractive and comfortably furnished rooms of the Columbia Club give evidence that there is no lack of accommodations for social gatherings and enjoyment.

The many stores for all branches of business and the large fish firms are open examples of the thrift and industry among the inhabitants.

The easy access to the city proper by ferry and electrics are other proofs of its popularity as a business centre besides its excellent position on the water front.

In driving, the fishing establishments and wharves of Sayward Bros., William H. Wonson & Son, Benj. Witham, Shute & Merchant, Slade Gorton & Co., B. F. Allen & Co., George Dennis, William Parsons, 2d & Co., Samuel Montgomery & Bro., Ernest H. Wonson and William S. Wonson, give an idea of the business life in this section (from the "Head of the Harbor" to the "Square"), the firms being old and established houses. A word regarding the William S. Wonson firm. It rests on a spot historic in marine circles as the place where the first schooner was built and launched by East Gloucester's noted settler in the early days, one Capt. Andrew Robinson. History tells us he "was the first contriver of schooners," which shows how much we are under obligation to East Gloucester's settler.

On launching his craft, as it went off the stocks a looker-on cried, "O how she scoons!" and Capt. Robinson, dashing a bottle of rum against the side of the vessel cried, "A scooner let her be!" (Later spelled schooner.) No maritime vocabulary of a date prior to 1713 mentions such a name for a vessel. Thus East Gloucester's old settler, Capt. Andrew Robinson, came rightly by the honor history gives him, and the spot whence his schooner was launched a notable one in this suburb's points of interest.

Passing by this historic wharf property, in a moment's drive we reach another picturesque point, one more marine view of Rocky Neck—the landing of the steam ferry "Little Giant," the steamboat wharf across the harbor where lands our handsome new steamer "Cape Ann," which plies between Gloucester and Boston, the fine fishing establishment of Reed & Gamage. Should a knight of the brush chance to be with you as you ride by this spot at sunset, he would be more than enthusiastic at the gorgeous colorings of the sky, which invariably occur at that time. This pier, for that reason, is more than a popular place for sketching by our resident artists during the summer.

Then imagine this scene in winter—the harbor frozen, the sea-gulls crying over the mast-heads, the ice-bedecked vessels and the grey snowy skies.

Right here we get a picturesque view of verdant hill land. On its heights are situated one or two houses—one especially by its odd structure and gaily colored paint at once attracts attention, the residence of Mr. Amos Story. The rocky height to the left of this house and almost opposite the fish firm of Reed & Gamage, is known as the "Bonfire Rock," for from time immemorial every Christmas eve the young people here have had their bonfire on this rock for the purpose of burning old Santa Claus out from his hiding place.

Thus driving along we are bounded on the left by hill land and on the right by wharf property, eventually reaching the firm of John F. Wonson & Co., at once recognized by the huge sea serpent nailed against their building, which was captured by one of their fleet on a recent voyage (?) This firm, besides being famed as the owner of this sea serpent, are also noted as being part owners of the "Rigel," which rescued the explorers, scientists and crew of the ill-fated steamer "Miranda," in the summer of 1894, in the Arctic ocean, the "Rigel" being engaged in the herring fishery off the coast of Greenland. Genuine and heartfelt thanks have been evinced by the rescued party to Capt. Dixon and his crew in more than an ordinary way. One of the party has written a book containing the story of their voyage home on the vessel, and the publication is handsomely illustrated.

Rocky Neck looms up after leaving the "Square," and it would be well to drive across the causeway when we reach it and visit another flourishing section of East Gloucester.

Rocky Neck will, this season, enter her name on the list as a summer resort. Mr. Frank Foster, a retired sea captain, has added an annex to the "Rackliffe House" on Fremont street, the old homestead of his wife's parents, which commands a beautiful view of the outer harbor, Ten Pound Island, Magnolia and Fresh Water Cove. and with its other natural quaint surroundings and extensive grounds, its proximity to the electrics and ferry, and its short distance from the resorts at Eastern Point, promises to become an enviable and attractive retreat for summer visitors.

The business establishment here of Messrs. James G. Tarr & Bro. will at once claim attention, as it comprises one of the largest out-fitting establishments in the city, where the fisheries in all its branches are conducted, from the landing of the fish to the curing, packing and shipping to all parts of the country. Here are their marine railways, on which the once fastest yacht, the "Mayflower," is seen every summer, besides many other sailing and steam yachts, being capable of repairing all sorts of crafts, as their

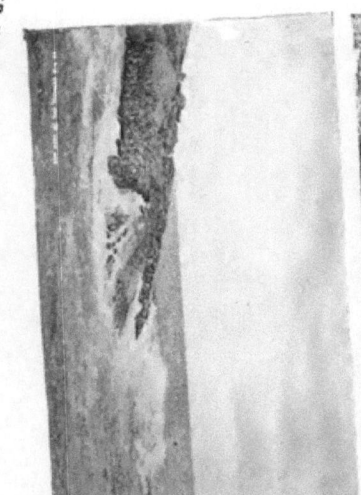

GLOUCESTER HARBOR.

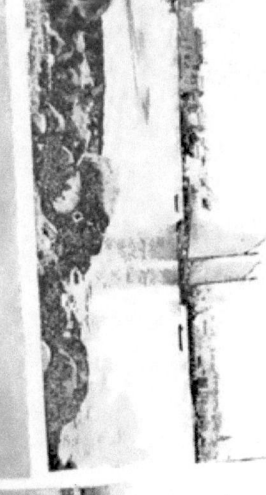

EXTREME OF CAPE ANN.

HALIBUT WHARF.

railways have all the latest improvements, giving employment to a large number of hands.

The copper paint factories of Messrs. Tarr & Wonson and James H. Tarr are other branches of business conducted here. These paints are as staple as flour, and have won their way into popular favor solely on their own merits.

The scene from this section is very fine, and will enchain the attention, as new and beautiful views attract the eye during the drive.

It may be well to state right here that in 1849 an undivided half of this entire property was purchased by Mr. Cyrus Story for $500. It was then used as a sheep pasture.

Ride to Eastern Point.

AGAIN crossing the causeway, we turn to the right, driving up Patch's Hill, pass the Harbor View Hotel, with all its modern improvements, its fine beach for bathing and its long pier, the popular and fashionable boat landing and after-dinner promenade. This hotel is especially attractive to Washingtonians; notably among them being Major Powell, of the Bureau of Psychology, Etymology and Analogy, and author of great philosophic and scientific works of value; Jane Brigham Curtis, the noted Washington artist, who was commissioned last season to paint the portraits of our noted summer resident litterateurs, Rev. Herbert D. Ward and Elizabeth Stuart Phelps-Ward; and Parker Mann, another noted Washington artist. At this hotel in seasons past summered the present wife of ex-President Harrison, and also every spring a large contingent of Wellesley and Radcliffe College students spend the vacation of that season at this hotel.

An inspection of the interior of the Harbor View annex, built in the season of '95, would be interesting. It has the quaint smoking-room, where a most delightful smoke can be enjoyed, in the midst of which one would be prone to revel in thoughts of the olden times, as the furnishings and decorations are so much in accordance with bygone days. The brick fire-place, the old fashioned pictures, old fashioned reading table, all give the air that city-bred people so much covet. Another pleasure would be to visit the dining hall, and view the fine collection of old blue china belonging to Mrs. Osborne. A drive through the court by the hotel, and "The Terrace" will dawn upon your view in all the glory of its Dutch architecture.

The interior contains 25 guests' rooms, a sun parlor and a large ground floor parlor, 32 x 56, with great open fire-place and colonial mantle, vouched to be 150 years old.

The winding gallery stair-case is most artistic and the draped window on the landing is a very unique arrangement, privileging one to gaze down into the parlor upon the morning picture of life and beauty or out over the restless, seething sea. "The Terrace" commands one of the grandest views here, and the house itself is not outrivaled here for odd architecture and furnishings.

Mr. and Mrs. Walter F. Osborne are the host and hostess of this popular hostelry.

Then on the left hand side of the hill is noticed Merrill Hall, well remembered as Craig Cottage, and is managed in connection with Hawthorne Inn. The hall had the honor of entertaining the noted dramatist, Bronson Howard, and the Baltimore authoress, Miss

Anna Vernon Dorsey, last season, and attracts a fine and select class of people.

Next we come upon the fine remodelled residence of the heirs of the Patch estate.

A little farther on, the popular Delphine, where for season after season such noted persons as Prof. Geo. E. Whiting, Prof. Louis C. Elson, Walter L. Dean and Childe Hassom have watched the growth and popularity of their favored resort. The charming cottage opposite the Delphine has been called Hassom Cottage in honor of its noted occupant, Childe Hassom. The Delphine is under the management of Mr. and Mrs. Simpson Lyle, and has been greatly improved upon this season.

Now we reach the Patch Willows and Hawthorne Lane, where white capped nurses or nattily attired bicyclists are enjoying the beauty and restfulness of this shady, vernal road. Shall we keep on or turn down the lane?

Turn down the lane by all means. Don't say that when in Gloucester you never visited Hawthorne Inn, "the place where you see the right side of life," for it is the largest, gayest and most charming of this suburb's hostelries. Before reaching the Inn one has to drive down a lane bordered with drooping willow trees, through which can be seen at intervals bits of the harbor, which are being kissed by the noon-day sun, while on the other side of the lane are bright green

ROCKY NECK.

WITCH HOUSE.

fields, the pleasure ground of feeding cattle and a popular sketching resort of the artists.

Two new Queen Anne cottages greet the eye on the right hand side of the lane, and are the summer homes of Delphine guests. Then we come upon a miniature village comprising Hawthorne Inn and its cottages of varied architecture, namely, the Old Home, Manse, Seven Gables, Province House, Orchard Cottage, Baldwin Cottage, Wayside, Seminary Hall, Peabody Hall,—and the temple of enjoyment, the Casino.

When the Inn is reached, one will not wonder why it is so popular as a summer resort, for the grand ocean view it commands from its broad and extensive verandas and "decks," the artistic arrangement of the cottages and their charming and comfortable furnishings and adornments, together with the excellent management of Mr. George O. Stacy, its proprietor and owner—all these advantages have won for it a phenomenal popularity. It is the Mecca for all the young people of the summer colony, and the Casino, so dear to them, teems with memories of their gay and delightful social events. You will not be disappointed in your visit to the Inn, in the least, after you've taken a tour of its grounds and cottages and, you will have no cause to marvel why it is the rendezvous, season after season, of some 450 people, comprising Philadelphians, Washingtonians, Gothamites, Chicagoans, Bostonians, and in fact people from all over the country, and why such noted people as Richard Mansfield, Miss Rollwagon, Mrs. Bronson Rumsey, of Buffalo, N. Y., Miss Helen M. Knowlton, Messrs. Theodore Wendell, Metcalf, and Duvernick, that noted trio in the art world, Lucy Cannon, the Baltimore artist, Judge James Smith, the noted Buffalo (N. Y.) judge and philanthropist, the late noted New York artist, De Haas, and wife, Emma Thursby, Judge Bumpus, Prof. Emerton of Harvard University, Charles Richard Dodge of Washington (of the Department of Fibre and Invention) and wife, have found it a pleasure to inscribe their names on the Hawthorne Inn register.

Leaving the Inn we drive through the willows, and soon notice a sign which reads, "To the Fair View." One really ought to drive up the road, for this hotel with its orchard and green fields, with the hills for a background, has for two seasons past been the summer home of Rudyard Kipling and wife, and Mrs. Kipling's mother and daughter, Mrs. Balestire (mother of the noted author, Wolcott Balestier,) and Miss Josephine Balestier.

Also here have Frank Dempster Sherman, the noted New York poet, and Miss Lucy Conant, Boston's well known artist, season after season sought this as their summer retreat, besides other noted people, who have enjoyed the geniality and courtesy of the owner and proprietor, Mr. Thomas Renton. Having viewed Kipling's summer home we come down the Fair View roadway, noticing several cottages on our right in a bordering field near the water front.

We also notice on our left an unpretentious dwelling, yet one of the oldest residences here, that has afforded a summer home for hosts of tourists.

This is the Mailman Cottage, the summer home of the editors of *Poet Lore*, Lieut. Herald and family of the United States navy, and many other noted and influential people from the various cities in the union, have inscribed their names on its register.

The primitiveness of the house, the esteem and respect in which the hostess is held, has so endeared its patrons to her that year after year the same familiar faces for nearly twenty-five seasons have greeted her when the summer opens.

A roadway to the right with the gateway open, attracts the eye, and although so near the Eastern Point Associates' property, with its gate wide open, let's drive through the gateway to the left, where a most imposing cottage greets the eye, which has a decided atmosphere of newness about it.

This new cottage erected this spring rests on the rocky bluff where once rested the cottage of Mrs. Elizabeth Stuart Phelps-Ward, now moved away to the hills.

By gazing at this cottage, one can see what a view Mrs. Ward's commanded, namely, of Eastern Point, Niles' Beach, the broad harbor, Norman's Woe, the

Magnolia shore and all the other natural surroundings of beauty.

This new cottage on this noted site, belongs to Mr. Claflin of Hopkinton, Mass., (a relative of Ex. Gov. Claflin of Massachusetts). Also exists here, the first cottage ever occupied by Mrs. Ward, and now occupied by Prof. and Mrs. Clement Lawrence Smith of Harvard University.

Leaving this locality we pass through the gate, which stands at the entrance of the Eastern Point Associates' property, by its ivy covered stone Gate Lodge, and can now enjoy a drive along the broad, smooth road, which has been built at the upper edge of what has been known as Niles' Beach.

This is the main plaisance of the whole summer colony, for here we meet the bicyclists, the promenaders, the bathers, the yachters, the driving parties and the artists, all of whom make this their promenade.

To our left we notice the "Beachcroft," occupying a fine position on the upland adjoining the beach, which gets the finest ocean view of any hotel here, and all the advantages of boating and bathing. This hotel is under the supervision of Mr. and Mrs. Thomas E. Day, and has always been especially attractive to Buffalonians (N. Y.), such as Rev. Dr. Lobdell, the noted divine of that city, Judge Foster of the Buffalo *Commercial*, F. S. Duvernick, the noted sculptor, of Boston, and many others.

The cottage next the Beachcroft, erected in the

WILLOWS, ANNISQUAM.

spring of 1894, was occupied during that season by the noted German pianist, Carl Baermann, and wife, and last season by the Lindley Johnsons of Philadelphia.

Following the main road we notice next the cottage of Mr. John J. Stanwood, one of Gloucester's prominent business men. Its situation on the eminence at once attracts attention, for its odd and unique style of architecture, with its close proximity to the beach, the fresh water pond and Brace's Cove, causes it to be one of the most admired of the summer homes here.

Those who remember this property as the Niles Farm cannot but marvel at what the Eastern Point Associates have done in transforming a beautiful rural moorland and beach into an up-to-date summer resort with enough rustic environments left to have an added charm.

We now drive by the grove of silver-grey poplars, where rests some fatigued bicyclist enjoying a quiet smoke, the meanwhile drinking in the magnificent ocean view before him; or some resting nurse girl sewing diligently or reading while her little charge sleeps calmly, soothed to dreamland by the gentle summer breezes.

Now we have reached the fresh water pond, dotted with water lilies or other aquatic plants, and in the depths of which pickerel find a home, to the joy of those who are fond of fishing-rod, hook and line.

This pond has been an interesting subject for artists—for who could resist the temptation to reproduce this scene before him, if the least passion for the art divine exist within his soul—those drooping willows gently bending to the water's surface, where are mirrored their glances?

We come upon the farm-house, now, its spider-webbed piazza covered with brilliant blossoming nasturtiums. We look for the old-fashioned garden and barn—they are gone, and in their place progress and the *fin de siecle* adornments and surroundings are noticeable. Several years ago it was the only house here, and the old-fashioned exterior possesses an interior equally as antique, and when it passed into other hands it was leased as a summer home and studio to Reginald Cleveland Coxe, the noted artist and illustrator of so many of William Dean Howells' novels. Mr. Coxe is the son of Bishop Cleveland Coxe of the diocese of New York. Last season it was occupied by Messrs. Eisham and Faxon, New York artists, and makes an ideal summer home for the knights of the brush.

We now come upon the " stone woman," which Mrs. Elizabeth Stuart Phelps-Ward claims as her discovery. This freak of nature is best viewed at a distance for one to wonder why she bears that appellation. She is in reality an old granite post that helped to form a gate-way to an old barn, which was situated to the right of the old road, now but a path

OLD MOTHER ANN, EAST GLOUCESTER.

compared to the fine laid out road around the shore line, which will aid in continuing your drive. From a distance one would veritably believe that a figure of a woman with a shawl thrown over her head, gazing out to sea had been carved out of this granite post. If one is curious to view the "stone woman" more closely, get down from your carriage and walk to her and see how easily "Father Time" in his sculpturing can deceive us. She looks, in fact, like Lot's wife, another name that has been given her.

Continuing our drive along this beautiful shore road, we gain a view of the whole sweep of the harbor. We next visit the pier, view the various handsome residences which grace the broad avenues, belonging to Messrs. Farrington, Lewis and Miss Church, members of the Eastern Point syndicate, and the Messrs. Greenough, Gay and Kay, all being wealthy residents of Boston, and as we proceed, inhaling the fragrance of the flower-bedecked fields and roadsides, there dawns upon us the Eastern Point lighthouse, with its guardian "Mother Ann," that statue in the rocky cliff. To get the best view of this other remarkable freak of nature, the existence of which is now as well known as that of the "Old Man of the Mountain," in the New Hampshire mountains, drive past the lighthouse till you reach a slight elevation in the road, then you will exclaim, like every other visitor to this spot, "How wonderful!" The sight you gaze on will be as real as the accompanying picture, yet even more defined.

To the late Mr. William Thompson, a resident of the "Witch City," and a former summer resident here, are we indebted for the discovery of this remarkable natural curiosity.

After paying our homage to the "mother of our Cape," we have a delightful shore road before us ere our route terminates, for the owners of this property have laid out through the hills a continuous road, which gives one the privilege of passing Brace's Cove, its Bemo Ledges, another view of the fresh water pond, the life saving station, its gray pebbly beach—the haunt and home of the sea gulls—scenes reproduced time and again on our resident artists' canvases—a proof of their remarkable beauty and charm. Following the road we find ourselves on a high elevation which, when descended, gives a full view of the Stanwood cottage and the handsome new cottage of the Elliotts of St. Louis.

We now find ourselves on our homeward route, passing again through the gate of the lodge, and by the hotels once more. Reaching the Hassom cottage, a willow road will be noticed, and if we should care to spare the time to drive down it, we would soon come upon the quaint little summer home of Mr. and Mrs. Herbert D. Ward (Mrs. Elizabeth Stuart Phelps-Ward) set in a broad green field surrounded by the expanse of hills.

BASS ROCKS, EAST GLOUCESTER, WITH JUDGE SHERMAN'S COTTAGE.

Reluctantly leaving all these pleasant scenes, we return by the same road and trace our way along East Main street to Mt. Pleasant avenue, and drive slowly up the hill. Reaching its height, the city with her buildings, the inner and outer harbors and the bay, all are in view, and make the avenue a very sightly location for the many pretty houses which are situated on and off the avenue.

We pass the fine farm of Mr. George M. Wonson, and should we take the time to drive in the fir-tree bordered roadway, we would think we were not at the seaside but in the country. A view from the cupola of the great barn here, which is always open to visitors, would never be forgotten.

Soon we have the privilege of viewing the handsome residence and beautiful grounds of the mayor of our city, for East Gloucester's public-spirited and prominent citizen, Hon. David I. Robinson, has for a third term had this honor bestowed upon him. Next to his residence is the finely equipped engine house, and a little farther on Mt. Pleasant Cemetery, where are laid to rest many who have fought a good fight and whose memories will ever be cherished in this vicinity.

A turn to the right brings us to the summer homes of the Bass Rock colony and the site of the famous Bass Rock Hotel, which was burned on the night of the 25th of January, 1896.

Slowly approaching the coast line, where the sea

in all its majesty is dashing the white waves against the rocks which line the shore in all directions, piles upon piles of these monster rocks meet the vision, true signs of the glacier period, and the sea madly riots over them, gaining the best of the combat, crawling up their sides, swirling over their smooth surfaces, dashing and pounding, oh! so cruel and treacherous looking — but possessing a fascination which renders the scene one of weird beauty and attraction.

The view at this point is one of the best about the Cape. The waters of old ocean, with the white wings of hundreds of vessels sailing in all directions, the pleasure and freight steamers sending their smoke into the heavens, at once tell us why Gloucester has reached such a place in the maritime world. The twin lights of old historic Thatcher's Island stand sentinel like in their grandeur. We also see Milk and Salt Islands with their fishermen's huts, and Brier Neck with Gloucester's Coney Island beyond; Little Good Harbor Beach with its hosts of surf bathers and promenaders; the trestle over which the Long Beach cars, freighted with human beings, run to that beautiful spot, Long Beach, where the Casino and the hills and dales, massive bowlders and smooth beach afford amusement and delight to the thousands of pleasure seekers. Here are many cottages, also, occupied by out-of-town people.

We can cross the channel and get on Little Good

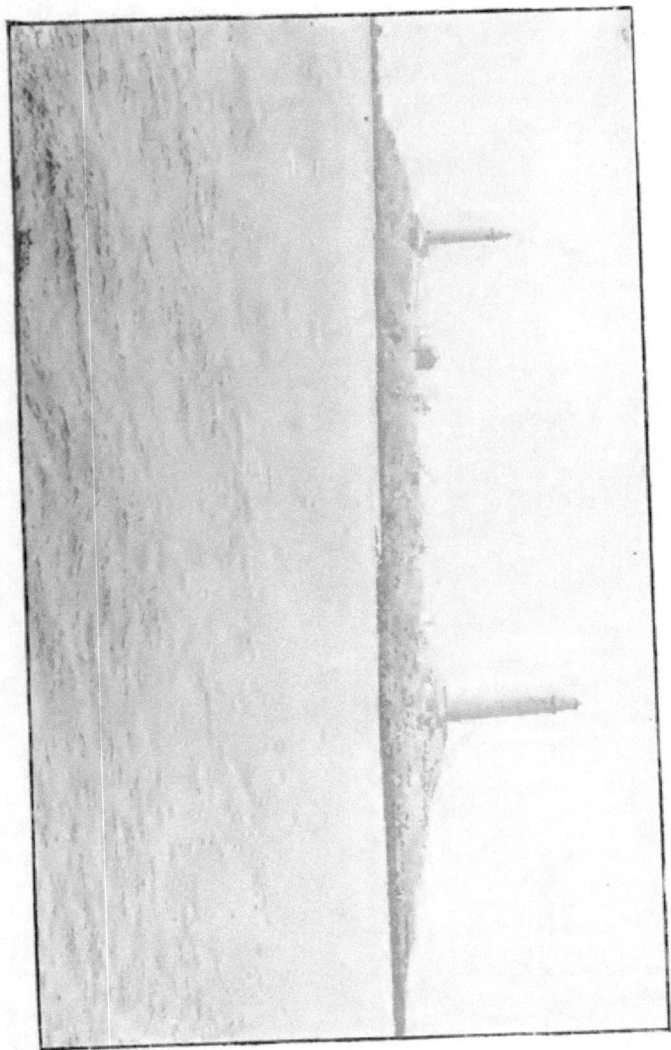

THATCHER'S LIGHTS.

SURF AND ROCKS, NEAR BASS ROCKS.

Harbor Beach, if the tide is sufficiently low, and ride over to Brier Neck and Long Beach if we wish, even to Rockport, a most delightful drive, with such a combination of magnificent scenery, flavored with salt water in all its absolute pureness.

As this drive has been very long, we are of the opinion that another day devoted to this route would be a fresher pleasure, therefore we turn into the quaint little "Joppa" road, drive along the Rockport road through that portion known as the "Farms," and return to our different destinations with such delightful impressions in our minds of East Gloucester, Mt. Pleasant avenue and Bass Rocks.

Drive to Magnolia.

ANOTHER popular and delightful drive is that to and around Magnolia.

Starting from the Surfside, we cross the Cut bridge, stopping a few moments to take in the fine harbor scene with Ten Pound Island, Eastern Point and Rocky Neck jutting out into old ocean, forming an attractive picture, while numerous vessels sailing in or out of the harbor, or gliding against the horizon, give life and animation to the grand panorama.

We turn to the other side of the bridge and we have a far different picture. Annisquam River winds in and out through the marshes, while towering above is Bellevue Heights, Wolf Hill with its camp houses and adjoining territory, forming a varied background to the scene, while in the distance West Gloucester, with its forests of pines, lends the charm of color and beauty.

On we go past the Stage Fort property, which Gloucester at one time was intent on purchasing as a park, but the generous bequest of Ravenswood, by the late Samuel E. Sawyer, will doubtless leave this beautiful and historic stretch of land for residential purposes.

MAGNOLIA POINT, (EAST), WITH BEACH, HOTELS, ETC.

An interesting incident occurred the summer when Buffalo Bill's troupe tented here and gave their wonderful exhibit. The Indians were more than charmed with the spot, and in their wanderings over the fields, miraculously came across mounds that were made by native Indians in the days of yore. Their chief immediately called them together and suitable commemorative services were held. It was certainly a very impressive picture when one watched them mount to the huge bowlders and shade their eyes and gaze out to sea, enveloped in their gaily colored blankets, for then one's imaginations were easily led to the historic days of our city, when men of their race really gazed from these headlands and watched the new settlers sail into the harbor and supplant them.

Driving past Stage Fort we ascend Bray's Hill and soon reach the residences of Messrs. John W. Bray and Charles B. Presson, on Beachmont avenue, which are worthy of favorable comment, as are the many valuable building lots for which these fertile fields will be used in the future.

On the opposite side of the road from Beachmont avenue we notice a little road, almost a cow path, which leads to Bond's Hill, where rests the hut of Gloucester's hermit, Mr. Mason A. Walton, who for years has lived in these dense woods far from all habitation, cultivating the friendship of birds, squirrels, woodchucks, spiders and other natives, which claim this spot *their* home. No more interesting place to visit (on foot) is there than this of hermit Walton's and no more intelligent person to converse with can be found. The hermit devotes his time to literary works of a botanical and political nature, from which his livelihood is gained. He sleeps nearly the year round in a hammock in a duck covered tent among the trees. He comes into town daily to dine, and is a familiar personage on our streets, usually attired in the conventional deep black, large slouched hat, under which rests a head well covered with sandy hair, and being lame, is always accompanied by a heavy walking stick. Having the hermit well placed in our imaginations and also an intention to visit him, we drive along, eventually reaching the Dale and Hovey estates, with their wealth of beauty and delightful woodland environments, enhanced still more by the Swiss style of architecture of their summer homes.

Just beyond and a little below the hill rests the former summer home of the late Samuel E. Sawyer, an attractive English villa, bearing the most appropriate appellation of "Brookbank." How much is our city indebted to the deceased owner of this villa, for the Sawyer Free Library and the funds for its maintenance, and for other gifts to our city, beside Ravenswood, which under the skilful handling of landscape gardeners will be in the near future Gloucester's park.

Then we have the drive along Fresh Water Cove to enjoy, and soon enter the famous wooded road with its agreeable shade and lovely tints of green, so restful on a bright, sunshiny day.

Here we meet the fine equipages and equestrians, which are proofs of the fashionable resort which we soon are to have the pleasure of visiting.

We take this leisurely and in good time arrive at the road which branches from the main road and leads to Magnolia. The sign board on the left informs us that Magnolia is reached by the avenue bearing its name. We turn into this avenue, obtaining glimpses of ocean scenery and the village, which is a foretaste of what is to come.

On we ride past pleasant cottages and the little chapel whose history speaks so eloquently of the religious sentiment of the natives of what was at the time it was erected known as Kettle Cove, until the name blossomed out into the more euphonious one of Magnolia, called such from those large, white, fragrant flowers which grow in the great tree covered swamps beyond the Magnolia hills.

Magnolias were discovered here by Dr. Cutler and are found in no other spot in New England, and thus proved very suggestive for a name for this summer resort.

The chapel here is very dear to the hearts of the people, especially to the elderly ones, as within its walls their prayers and songs of praise have rendered it a consecrated place. Here they have gathered year after year when their hearts have been made heavy by the hand of affliction, and found comfort in God's promises, and in their hours of joy they have been rendered still the happier, as they participated in the services of this sanctuary.

Across the way is the schoolhouse, and near by is the old graveyard, where the form of many a loved one has been recently laid to rest.

On we drive, passing the Oak Grove House, which is charmingly situated a little off the avenue, in a grove of sturdy oaks, which give it its name. Then we come to Willow Cottage, famous as the first public house in Magnolia to entertain strangers within its hospitable walls. Crescent Beach lies to the right, where at the regular hour for bathing, two hundred people may be seen enjoying their salt sea bath, and the Crescent Hotel, owned by Mr. Allen Knowlton, has a deserved popularity among those who wish to obtain the benefits and enjoy the pleasures of a well conducted seaside resort. Many from New York and Philadelphia have made this their summer home for years.

The far famed Hesperus House on Hesperus avenue, is an object of much attraction. It was built by Mr. Daniel Fuller in 1877, since which time it has been much enlarged. It is under the management of Mrs. Ora Page, and has secured a reputation which fills it season after season with the wealthy and refined from all parts of the country, and its parlors and

dance hall are centres of nearly all the social events of the Magnolia summer colony.

Opposite the Hesperus House is the handsome Hesperus Villa, a well appointed lodge, owned by Mrs. Octavia Wilkins of Brooklyn, N. Y., and where many lodgers from the Hesperus House find a spacious and lovely artistic summer home.

The Oceanside on Lexington avenue is another attractive and first-class hotel, under the management of Mr. George A. Upton. It commands a charming view of ocean and forest, and the sojourner at this establishment will find his wants well cared for and will have opportunities of meeting celebrities in art, music and letters, and noted people in the financial and social world, which proofs can be found on the Oceanside register.

Next looms up the Magnolia Hotel, a magnificent hostelery, inviting all who wish for a charming summer resort to try the merits of its pleasant rooms and social life. It makes a long needed addition to the hotel accommodations of Magnolia, and under the management of Mr. H. W. Priest is gaining an enviable reputation among the popular hotels.

Riding over these beautiful avenues, which everywhere abound, inhaling the air, toned up with salt sea breezes, the eye ever charmed with the changing scenes of ocean, beach, forest, well kept grounds and lawns, handsome dwellings, and all the accompaniments that wealth and refinement can achieve, it can hardly be conceived that all these changes have been effected within the past fifteen years. But such is the fact. The work of laying it out was commenced by its owner, the late Daniel W. Fuller, of Swampscott, in 1867. Then it was simply a fishing hamlet. It was a work of slow growth, but perseverance won, and the Hesperus House, of which he and his wife were the original proprietors, together with the sale of building lots and continued good management on the part of those who have had charge of the property after Mr. Fuller's untimely death by falling down a mine in Denver, Col., in 1880, have brought the place to its now well deserved state of prosperity, and its future has a most brilliant forecast.

Nor is Magnolia popular alone as a summer resort, but also for natural and famous points of interest— the Flume, Rafe's Chasm, and Norman's Woe, and the drive around the Point. These are attractions at this beautiful place that are worthy of attention. When one drives round the Point, the road skirts the very edge of the water, in fact, you seem right out in the ocean, with all sizes of sailing and steam craft passing and repassing, the waves dashing against the stalwart boulders, all combining to make an enjoyable ride and picturesque also. The Flume is a channel in the cliff of the rocky shore leading from the Flume road, which can boast of a length of 150 feet and a width of 40 inches, with its sides almost perpendicular. Near by is that ravine, Rafe's Chasm, into

RAFE'S CHASM, MAGNOLIA.

which the waters of the ocean roll with terrific force. It is a deeply cut fissure into the solid ledge extending inward 200 feet, with a depth of 60 feet, and a width ranging from 3 to 15 feet. Just after a storm, one should visit here and witness a grand spectacle, for when the waves dash into the chasm you can hear a noise resembling thunder.

Rafe's has claimed one victim, as the iron cross here signifies. Miss Martha Marion of Walton, N. Y., was swept off the rocks into the chasm in 1879, by the treacherous waves, and the summer residents erected the cross here to her memory.

Following the path here one soon comes upon the reef of Norman's Woe, a small island of solid rock situated a few hundred yards from the main land. Norman's Woe at once recalls Longfellow, who has given it such a world fame in his "Wreck of the Hesperus," which occurred off this reef in the latter part of the seventeenth century.

The homeward drive is along the road through the woods, which proves a most delightful experience, giving, as it does, a diversity of scenery replete with pleasure. The road leads to the main highway, and a turn to the right will soon bring you back to the Surfside whence you started.

Around the "Little Heater."

A MOST delightful drive is that formerly known as around the "Little Heater," now Magnolia avenue; it affords much pleasure and is very popular. Starting on Western avenue, you turn into Essex avenue, if you choose, but you can vary the ride by continuing along Western avenue until you reach Bond street, and you will find that this will afford an inviting drive, shady and clean. It connects with Essex avenue just above Lovett's hill. This Bond street drive is a great favorite, and for a short one combines much to commend it.

Continuing along Essex avenue, and after passing the abutment of the Boston and Maine Railroad, you turn to the left at the foot of the hill and notice the brick pumping station of the Gloucester Water Works. Here commences your journey through the woods, and a most delightful experience it proves, winding in and out under the grateful shelter of the trees.

The road is not very wide, but is in good condition, and is about four miles in length with plenty of turn-outs at convenient distances to allow the passing of teams. One need not hurry on this road, as you should take your own time and thoroughly enjoy it. There are plenty of opportunities for strolling in the woods, picking wild flowers and ferns, and in their season the luscious berries.

One caution is necessary. Time yourself so as not to be on the West Gloucester end when the cars are due, as the railroad track in that section runs for a considerable distance very near the highway, and if you have a spirited horse an unpleasant experience might be yours should you meet the train. After once going over the route and having a time table, this can be avoided, and should not detract from the pleasures of the drive.

The "Little Heater" road terminates at Magnolia, and you can cross the main road and enjoy a drive in this section, returning over the road through the woods previously spoken of, or the road may be retraced and the drive home can be taken over Western avenue, which is considered among the finest in this vicinity.

"Around the Parish."

THROUGH Essex avenue, from its junction with Western avenue, to Concord street, West Gloucester, and here your ride "Around the Parish" commences, which will take you overs ome four or five miles of good road which almost encircles the larger part of the old Second Parish of Gloucester. The traveller can turn either to the east or west, arriving at the end of the ride again at the starting point, the guide-board pointing the way to "Essex," "Wingaersheek Beach" and "Willoughby Park."

We will turn to the left down Concord street, the road that leads to the pleasant summer houses at Presson's Point, just beyond which stands the Bray school house, while directly opposite are its two predecessors, one its original size and the other considerably enlarged, both used as dwellings.

Farther on, Thompson street or "Old Meeting House road" turns to the left, and Causeway street to the right leads the way to Russ' Island; then where Atlantic street turns towards Wingaersheek Beach, keep the left hand road past the late Judge Thompson's summer residence, and then the way winds amidst pleasant pasture and woodland, by green fields and flourishing gardens, with now and then a farm house showing among its orchard trees, and then to the right the view broadens and Wingaersheek and Ipswich beaches with their white sands gleaming brightly in the sun, and glimpses of the blue waves of the ocean, with here and there a sail, meet the eye. Westward winds Essex river with Conomo Point and Cross' Island and their cottages in full view, while several ways turn from our road to the pleasant camps of numerous summer residents who every year make the north shore of West Gloucester their homes.

Then at the foot of a steep hill we come to the northwesterly end of Thompson street, the eastern extremity of which we passed several miles back. On this street, a few rods from Concord street, is the "Old Burying Ground," one which will call to the mind of the visitor Whittier's exquisite poem, which seems so well to describe this ground:

"The winding wall of mossy stone frost flung and broken, lines
A lonesome acre thinly strewn with grass and wandering vines.
Without the wall a birch tree shows its drooped and tasselled head,
Within a stag horned sumach grows, fern leaved with spikes of red."

There on the verdant hillside is the grave of Rev. Samuel Tompson, the first pastor of the old second church, whose home, fast falling to decay, is just beyond, and whose "meeting house" stood a few rods still farther, where its foundation stones can scarcely be seen. Years after, his name was given to the road where stood his church and home and where to-day his grave is green with waving grass and bright with summer wild flowers. We give an illustration of his tombstone, with the inscription thereon:

Still onward our path takes us by the road that leads to the crumbling grist mill, and then the road divides to the right over Walker's Creek by a wooden bridge. Concord street continues to Essex line, and just as the boundary stone is passed, a way to the right leads to the summer houses of Conomo Point, one of the fairest locations on our north shore; or a few rods more and turning sharply to the left you are soon on Essex avenue, which you will reach earlier if you prefer to turn through Sumner street and ride past Andrews' cider mill, Burnham's saw mill and many pleasant homes and gardens.

On Essex avenue you ride easterly, and something like a mile and a half from the junction of Summer street, past the Congregational church, the post-office and the Universalist church, will bring you again to Concord street. If you wish to vary your ride, the rough but pleasant wood-shaded path of Ferndale, the hilly Bray street, or Lincoln or Walker street, each have their beauties; indeed, these rides through West Gloucester, "Around the Parish," to Wingaersheek Beach, and walks through her pastures and woodlands are among the pleasantest on Cape Ann.

Mount Anne or Thompson's Mountain is one of the important features of West Gloucester. This is the highest elevation in this section of Essex County, and a fine view can be obtained from its summit. Just below lie the the woodland farms and homesteads of West Gloucester, and beyond, Gloucester harbor and city, Riverdale, Annisquam, Magnolia, Wingaersheek and Ipswich beaches, Essex and other neighboring towns. To the south is Massachusetts bay, and beyond the dome of the State House, Bunker Hill with its monument, the blue hills of Milton, and as the eye follows the horizon westward, far away, may be seen Mount Wachusett; northward the mountains of New Hampshire and the blue peak of Agamenticus; and eastward the ocean with its white sails. The road from Essex avenue is for the most part a pretty, shaded woodland path, about two hundred yards from the post office.

West Gloucester, Willoughby Park and Wingaersheek Beach.

WEST GLOUCESTER has every indication of becoming as popular and attractive as a seaside resort as any other of the standard resorts in and about Gloucester, for in its precincts are situated the famous Willoughby Park and Wingaersheek Beach, which remain in all their historical and marvellous beauty, no inroads upon their natural charms having been permitted.

To reach West Gloucester you drive along Western avenue, across the bridge, then turn to the right across Essex avenue, up the hill, passing the sightly residence of William A. Pew, Esq., with its commanding prospect; also the charming residence and farm at Edgewood belonging to Mr. Samuel G. Pool. A little farther on is the extensive building of the Russia Cement Co., and soon is seen the spacious ice house belonging to Mr. Francis W. Homans at Fernwood Lake, which it will be well to visit. A short ride further, and you may cross the railroad track on the right and leave the regular highway, passing through Fernwood with its many attractions.

Here it is that Major David W. Low has made for himself a delightful suburban home, where he lives the year round, while most of the other buildings are for summer homes only. Among these are the residences of Charles H. Pew, Esq., George W. Somes, Miss Elizabeth Saville, Edwin O. Parsons, Hiram Rich, Elias P. Burnham, Joseph Rowe, Allie Somes, Joseph M. Parsons, Austin D. Elwell, Will Perkins, George Todd, D. S. Watson, Fred. Pearce, Mrs. Charles Pearce, William Presson, Edward L. Rowe, Daniel H. Wallace, Charles Gardner, John D. Haskell of Lynn, and William McKechnie of Boston. These houses nearly all front Little River, and excelcellent facilities for boating, bathing, etc., are close at hand.

Turning to the left near the residence of Charles H. Pew, you drive to Stanwood's Point, on which many summer cottages are built. The old Stanwood mansion is still standing, and is utilized by Mr. Fred. L. Stacy as a summer residence. The Point has many attractions, giving fine views of West Gloucester, Russ' Island, Presson's Point, Annisquam river and the city proper. Retracing your way, you keep to the right, through Fernwood, and emerge a little beyond the railroad station, and turning to the right pass the head of Little River. The ancient house on the left is 200 years old, and for many years was used as a tavern. It is said to have been built by Jacob

Davis, a grandson of one of the first settlers of that name on Cape Ann.

Soon we reach Concord street on the right, and turning thereon travel directly to the seashore. This drive is full of interest. You pass by thriving farms and as you climb the hills get glimpses of varied and beautiful scenery. In due time we reach the residence of Mr. Amos L. Garland, formerly the summer home of the lamented Charles P. Thompson, Esq., nearly opposite which is Atlantic avenue. This you enter, and the beauties of the drive grow more and more entrancing. Passing slowly up the hill, the top is gained and a scene of surpassing loveliness and beauty breaks upon the view. The waters of Annisquam river, flowing from Ipswich bay to Gloucester harbor, wind in and out so cool and inviting; Pearce's Island, Thurston's Point, Russ' Island, Wheeler's Point, Riverdale and Annisquam present their attractions; while the yachts on the river's bosom glide hither and thither, which with the row boats and their merry occupants give life to the scene. The eye never tires of the beautiful panorama of earth, sky and water, so charmingly intermingled.

Descending the hill the road carries you along the river's bank, and you pass the farm house of Mr. Isaac J. Proctor, then the farm of Dr. George Morse with its attractive outlook, thence on by the stone pier 1200 feet in length, extending to low water mark, affording a landing at all times of tide, then the

quarry, and in a short time you are at the entrance of Willoughby Park. Adjoining is the entrance to the Wingaersheek property owned by E. C. Hawkes, Esq., of Buffalo, New York, comprising some 400 acres, which the owner is constantly improving and which bids fair of proving one of the finest watering places on the coast. Two elegant stone cottages and one of wood have been erected on the "Loaf," and the future of this magnificent piece of property is most promising.

Willoughby Park is a portion of the Coffin farm, which was settled by one Peter Coffin in 1688, his father purchasing it from a Londoner (England) named Willoughby; it comprises about 200 acres of that charming and quaint village of West Gloucester, and is a continuation of the far-famed belt of fashionable seashore resorts—Nahant, Swampscott, Beverly Farms, Marblehead Neck, Manchester-by-the-Sea, Magnolia, Pigeon Cove, and Bay View, terminating with Wingaersheek Beach on Ipswich Bay, at the mouth of Essex and Annisquam rivers.

This high tract of land is rich in heavy wooded forests of birch, oak, pine and walnut; beautiful ravines, and towering hills and knolls, which give unobstructed views of Ipswich Bay with all its picturesque marine beauty, the winding rivers of Essex and Annisquam and the tall spires and roofs of the city of Gloucester. It is an ideal spot for a summer home, for you can indulge in all the sports unrestricted to which the present generation are devoted, such as gunning, fishing, rowing, sailing and bathing, the facilities being unsurpassed; and for a bicycle or horse-back ride, what can be compared to that two-mile stretch of hard, white sand of Wingaersheek Beach?

The walks over the Park are delightful, for then you can observe and study the curious formation of rocks and granite, mount the grass-covered sand dunes and revel in their charms, gather the beautiful wild flowers and luscious wild berries which grow in profusion, and gaze into the calm, unruffled depths of Sleepy Hollow Lake.

The Park is but five minutes drive from Wingaersheek Beach, which is one of the finest on the New England coast, being two miles long and 600 feet wide at low water; its hard, clean, sandy surface free from debris, looks like a great marble floor, and is admirably adapted for riding, walking and bathing, as one can readily conceive. One or two wrecks half buried in the sand awaken at once our imaginations and poetic tendencies and give us immediate ideas of the nature of the "Storm King" when he visits this coast.

It is fascinating to watch the waves rippling in, their white foam caressing the fair sands and wreathing them with snowy laces; at other times we gaze awe-struck, as we perceive the huge billows baffling with the elements or cannonading the fortress of the

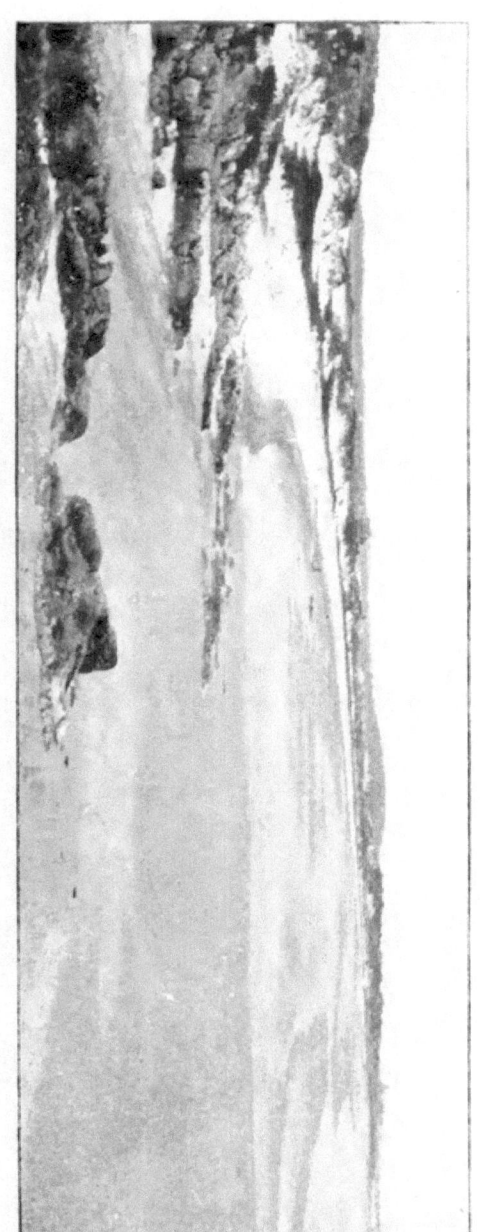
WINGAERSHEEK BEACH.

land, their echoes dying away behind the sand dunes, which gives a weird aspect to the whole scene.

To the right may be seen old Annisquam and the cottages of that summer colony from Cambridge, Mass., and you get a glimpse of rocky Bay View and the broad Ipswich bay, of Newburyport and Portsmouth, N. H., and even the distant shores of Maine; on a very clear day, towering high on the horizon, Mount Agamenticus may be seen, and the late Celia Thaxter's home, the Isles of Shoals.

The Park's proximity to Boston is an added advantage, for in twenty minutes you can reach the West Gloucester station, and have the choice of eleven trains to carry you to any station on the Boston and Gloucester route throughout any summer day, for Boston is but 27 miles from West Gloucester, and only one hour and twenty minutes ride.

A road in the Park, a mile and a quarter in length, furnishes a drive from Bray street to the Atlantic avenue entrance, also direct to the beach. You are near Gloucester also, and can reach the city proper by the electrics, which pass by Concord avenue about every fifteen minutes. You can also visit Essex, Hamilton, Beverly and Ipswich by this electric route.

Therefore, let one go to Willoughby Park, wander from point to point in this beautiful preserve, and he will find in its environments and contiguous cities and towns all that will satiate the physical, pleasurable and spiritual needs of one looking for a first-class summer resort. In this charming bit of country one will find beauty everywhere as the eye ranges far and wide over the landscape.

As one finds in its bracing air that which is healthful, there is something also in the atmosphere that reaches to the mind and heart, that is inspiriting and helpful. Nature at all times is in communication with an impressionable spirit, and here one may draw inspiration for grander achievements in life, and forget for the moment the dull rumble of the wheel of fortune and cling closer to the purer, sweeter, holier thoughts of one's inmost soul.

This Park property is owned by the Messrs. Procter Brothers and Dr. George Morse, of Gloucester, who will furnish descriptive circulars and plans to any who desire them. It is ready for purchasers.

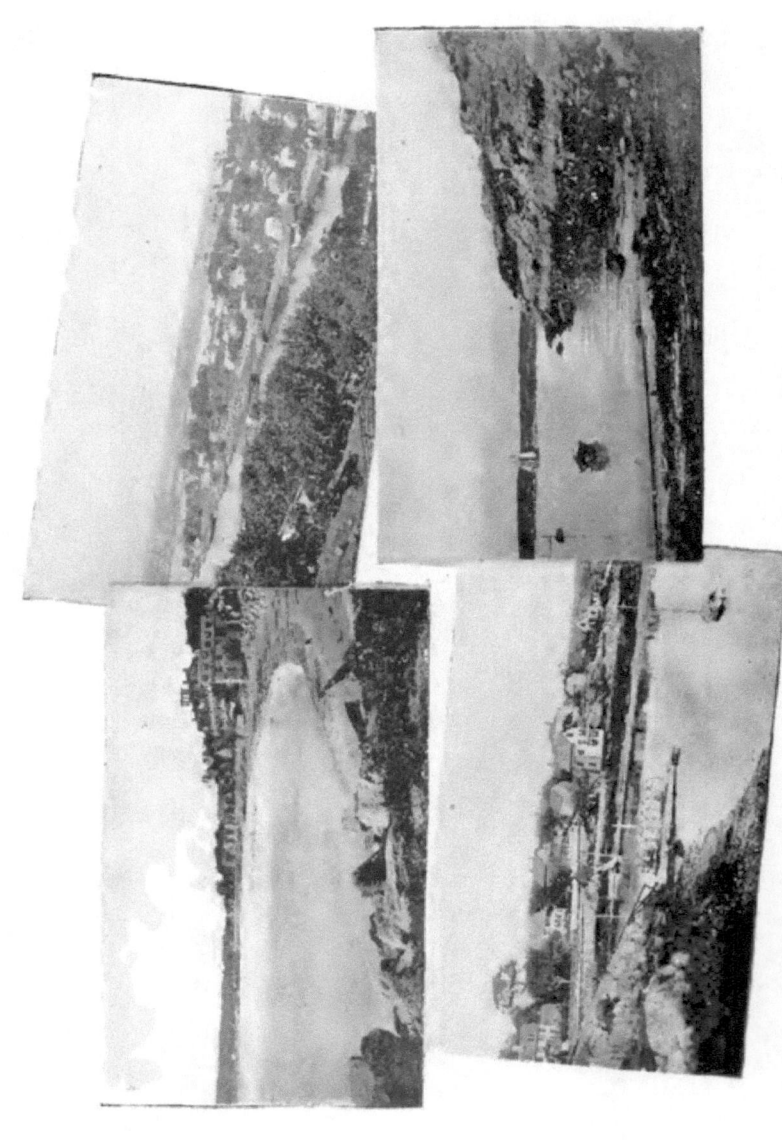

PAVILION BEACH. BENT'S LANDING, ANNISQUAM. ANNISQUAM. ROCKY NECK.

Around the Cape.

"AROUND the Cape," as it is called, gives one a fifteen mile drive replete with pleasure.

Taking the Surfside as our starting point, if we choose, we progress along Washington street, passing the Boston & Maine Railroad station, and proceed through a section attractive by its neat and well kept residences, past Oak Grove Cemetery, the resting place of the noted singer, Emma Abbott Wetherell, and husband, and where a beautiful monument to their memory is one of the features of note in this city of the dead.

Soon we get glimpses on the left of the Annisquam River near the bridge with its fleet of yachts at anchor, a portion of Wolf Hill and Russ' Island, with Little River and Fernwood; then on the right are the handsome residences of City Clerk John J. Somes, Mr. Horace A. Smith, Hon. William W. French, Messrs. Augustus F. Cunningham, David B. Smith, Wilbur Locke, Ezra Phillips, Alphonso Tarr; and now the Ellery homestead, the oldest house in Gloucester, memorable as being the residence of Rev. John White, dawns upon our view at the head of the creek. It is an old-time dwelling-house indeed, for it was erected in 1717, and when shown over its interior no doubts will be entertained as to its antiquity.

Next we pass the "Green," another historical spot in Gloucester's annals, then the Gilbert Hospital, the public gift of another of Gloucester's generous hearted citizens, the late Addison Gilbert. Here are the Babson, Allen, Low, Brown and Pearce residences and estates, together with others which have sheltered the old and highly respected Gloucester families, and they with commendable pride keep them in good condition and occupy them; thus they are fitting memorials of the struggle it cost to place Gloucester on its present strong foundation.

We are now in Riverdale, so appropriately named, and pass the massive ledge of granite known as the "Poles." Reaching the Mill, which for many years has continued its grinding, a fine and picturesque view is obtained of the water-course known as the Mill Creek, and from which its motive power is derived. It is fascinating to watch it as it curls in and out above the dam, rolling up beyond the Babson farm to the Allen farm with the ebbing of the tide, while below it courses to the Annisquam River.

Here is a monument erected to the memory of those from this section who laid down their lives for their country. To the left is the attractive road leading to Wheeler's Point, a popular summer resort of many well known campers. Slowly up the hill

we go, by the M. E. Church, and while ascending the hill we must not fail to notice the large boulder near Hillside Hall, which has a very perfect resemblance of a dog's head, as seen at a short distance. The nose points to the eastward, and a crack in the ridge gives an excellent fac simile of the animal's eye, which appears as if closed, while the general shape of the rock is a realistic representation. Then as we drive we catch charming views of Ipswich Bay, sand dunes and rivers; we pass through the famous Willow Road, by Sunset Cottage, owned by Mr. William G. Brown, thence by Hodgkins' mill, with its picturesque settings, note Dr. Wetherell's villa and its lovely situation, then reach Goose Cove, and driving briskly soon reach the bridge at Lobster Cove, which we cross, and the pretty village with its Indian name, Annisquam, is before us, where much will be found to engage attention.

At the first crossing of the bridge, a fine view of Wheeler's Point, Pearce's Island with its shores dotted with summer houses, and the marshes and creeks on the opposite side flanked by the West Gloucester hills, presents scenes of surpassing beauty, and we at last realize why artists in numbers innumerable just revel in their profession while here.

Close down to the river's side, at Annisquam Point, built on the solid rock, is the quaint cottage of Mr. George J. Marsh. Its location is unsurpassed for catching the cool breezes and for the grand sweep of maritime loveliness afforded by the river and bay, and you can step into your dory or pleasure boat directly from the rocks. The house is fitted up expressly for pleasure and comfort—a combination devoutly wished for in this world of ours, and here you have it. Swinging beds and other devices for comfort invite when weary, and all that is needed for genuine pleasure and restfulness is here dispensed with lavish hospitality. It is the ideal spot for keen enjoyment, being close at hand to the fishing grounds and directly in the path of the birds as they take their southward flight. The interior arrangements are so quaint and comfortable that we feel perfectly at home beneath its hospitable roof.

Norwood Heights is a most attractive summer resort, having been laid out and improved for building lots in the summer of 1895. Several dwellings are already erected and others have been contracted for. It is most advantageously located in the centre of the village, very easy of access, and commands a fine view of Ipswich Bay and its beautiful surroundings. It is under the management of Mr. Frank Bott and Mr. Fred. Norwood.

The visit to the Cambridge settlement and the Grand View House and the other famous hostelries here gives opportunities to obtain magnificent views of river and ocean scenery and make such delightful impressions upon us that we feel compelled to linger and admire, but as we are bound around the Cape we

promise ourselves to come again and oft to this quaint and attractive retreat, and pursue our way through the village, with its dwellings and quiet, inviting appearance, reaching the road leading to the Cove, passing the Annisquam Universalist Church, which stands like a sentinel in white at the junction of the roads and reflecting great credit upon the sturdy and self-sacrificing men and women of 1831, upwards of sixty-five years ago, whose efforts built it, and on a Sabbath it would be a pleasant place to visit and join in the services.

Continuing a short distance we approach the beautiful summer residence of Col. and Mrs. Jonas H. French. The gate is wide open inviting us to drive in, and we do so and enjoy the delights of a well kept lawn and garden, which in summer time abounds in beautiful flowers, some very rare, affording delight to the many who avail themselves of the hospitable spirit of these dwellers by the sea, who are so willing to share that which affords so much pleasure to them with the public.

We pass from here to the grounds of the late Gen. B. F. Butler's home by the seashore, enjoying the beautiful maritime picture so lavishly exhibited, and are soon on the main road again, where the sound of the clicking of the drills of the Bay View stone workers betokens busy life and activity.

Bay View is a pleasant village, having a Methodist church, which is well sustained. It has an artificial harbor made of immense blocks of stone, serving as a breakwater. There is also a United States Life Saving Station at Davis' Neck.

We now approach Lanesville by ascending a hill, on the brow of which stands the Catholic Church of the Sacred Heart. The village has a neat, restful appearance. Fishing and quarrying business form the principal sources of industry, and a goodly number of tourists enjoy the fine scenery and the healthful sea breezes. The people are most hospitable and social. It has a Congregational and a Universalist church, good school accommodations, and is a progressive place, and one which is increasing in population and importance.

Following the road as it winds along through the village centre, past the churches and the stores, hearing the click of the drills and occasionally the report of the blasts on the quarries, noticing the huge loads of granite being drawn toward the granite wharf of the harbor, which, like all others in this section, was the result of patient labor, the huge blocks of granite being piled up as a breakwater, the waves often proving so powerful as to start them from their resting places—we jog along through the village of Folly Cove and then to Pigeon Cove.

As we come up the valley past the hill-environed and pretty Glen Cove, the first prominent object that greets our vision to the right is the beautiful residence of Mr. and Mrs. J. E. Hartwell, who have given this

charming place the poetic name of "Interlodge." On the left the most prominent object is the old Babson farm house on the heights. The approach to the house is through an avenue of ancient elms that afford a grateful shade in the warm summer days and lend an additional charm to the surroundings. This house, with all its valuable land, some seventy or more acres, is the property of the Rockport Granite Company. An avenue on this property, which winds around by the ocean and through the fields, makes a walk or a drive in this vicinity one unsurpassed on the Cape for its grand view on sea and land.

Passing on we take a view of the beautiful Sunset Hill. This is a favorite resort for many of the summer visitors when day is departing to watch the last lingering radiance of the setting sun as it flushes wave and shore. Visitors to this vicinity will observe an ancient and weather-beaten gambrel-roofed house near Halibut Point; it dates far back into the misty past, and was in the early days the home of Samuel Gott, and is still occupied by his descendants; it is on high ground, and the view is a beautiful one. This old house and its picturesque surroundings have often been the subject for the artist's pencil and brush.

On the opposite side of the street, on an elevation overlooking the woods and valleys, as well as the waters of Ipswich bay, are a number of pretty summer residences.

From this point we turn down a slight declivity

and soon are among the avenues of Andrews' point; they were laid out by Messrs. Phillips and Babson, and contain many miles of very fine roads unsurpassed for walking, carriage or bicycle riding. Turning in on the main avenue, the first house of note we see is Oak Knoll, the elegant residence of Mr. Edwin Canney, who, with his family, resides here throughout the year. Another charming house built for permanent residence is the "Haven," the beautiful home of the late Mrs. Corinne H. Bishop.

Two of the most charming places on the Cape, if not on the Massachusetts coast, are the homes and their surroundings of Mr. John Stowell—beautiful "Meadowcliff"— and the Way villa, the home of the late J. M. Way, Esq. The latter is an elegant house built of granite, and is a very imposing structure.

Prof. Merrill, of the Boston Latin School, has a beautiful residence here; from the broad piazzas of his home can be seen the town of Rockport and also a grand view of Pigeon Hill, as well as the breakwater and Avery's Rock, of which the poet Whitter wrote that touching poem, "The Swan Song of Parson Avery."

Other beautiful cottages are the Frothingham, Chapin, Putnam, Barber, Wood, Willey, Emery, Thalemhier, Brooks, Brewer, Brewster, Millett, Phillips, Taft, Hosmer, Smith, and many others.

We hurriedly look over the pretty cottages and admire the graceful winding avenues, and soon are in

the vicinity of the hotels, the largest of which is the Pigeon Cove House. In 1866 Mrs. Norwood retired from the house, after keeping it acceptably many years. Mrs. Ellen S. Robinson took the house in 1871, as owner and hostess, and soon moved the old house from its site and built on the same spot a larger and more attractive one. It is a spacious and convenient building, and enjoys an excellent reputation.

In the same spring, too, the Ocean View House was erected and immediately opened for visitors. It is but a few minutes' walk from the Pigeon Cove House, and commands a fine view of the ocean. A large annex was subsequently built to this hotel.

Down on the extreme point, in a grand location, is situated the Linwood Hotel, and the ocean breezes and views enjoyed from its piazzas are much appreciated during the heated term.

A short distance from the hotels are boarding houses, among the more prominent being the Glen Acre, the Rose Lawn, Sunny Side, Sea View and Cedar Cottage, while many others take lodgers.

But we must not miss the old Garrison house, said to be one of the oldest (if not the oldest) houses on Cape Ann. It stands in a field bordering on Granite street, with some grand old trees in the yard. But a part of the edifice is more ancient than its venerable neighbors. The tradition is that this part was erected in 1692 by two young men as a safe retreat for their mother who had been proclaimed a witch. So far from the settlement of Salem, hidden in the deep woods, the misunderstood and persecuted woman was beyond reach of injury.

Joshua Norwood enlarged and improved this house and for some time made it his home. In 1740 he left it and moved to Gap Head; since then the old house has been several times modified by additions and adornings, so that it is admired for its comely, modern as well as its venerable features. Its thick oaken walls, low rooms, great corner posts and cross-beams, ample chimney and small window-frames, make it a pleasing contrast with the showy but less substantial dwellings built in the present day. Its extensions and verandas overrun with woodbine and flowering vines, and its dark paint, like weather stains, are in harmony with its older parts and its picturesque surroundings.

Let us now drive down Powsil Hill to the snug and safe harbor of Pigeon Cove. This harbor was badly damaged by the great storm of 1841. The wall (where now is the substantial breakwater) gave way and fell, and most of the vessels in the harbor were destroyed. Many marked improvements have been made at this harbor of late years. The Cape Ann Granite Company, of which Col. Jonas H. French is the head, have steam cars running direct from their inland quarries to the wharf in this harbor, and are doing a large business shipping stone to the breakwater and elsewhere. The Rockport Granite Company, S. N. Waite & Son, Mr. Edwin Canney, Mr. C. H. Cleaves, and others, also have many large vessels here to load almost daily, in fair weather, for New York, Philadelphia and other ports. This little village has five very pretty churches, which speaks well for its residents.

A few steps westerly from the harbor on a ledge overlooking the cove and bay, is a very ancient habitation called the Old Castle. Its back roof descends to within a few feet of the ground, and its upper story juts over the lower, in the manner of a block house. Its craggy site commands a fine prospect far out over the sea.

Some fifty-six years ago the following litterateurs of note sought this locality, namely: Richard H. Dana, Sr., who was the first visitor, and being so enthusiastic over its charms soon had his friend, "The Nestor of Poets," William Cullen Bryant, interested in the spot. He went there and reveled in its varied scenery. Then Ralph Waldo Emerson visited the place for a week, and on his return wrote that familiar poem, "Seashore," which gives one such an excellent idea of the favorable and delightful impressions the most distinguished of American essayists experienced while there and how they can be described in poetical language.

Thus since 1840 this village has been a most attractive resort, owing to its historical and natural points of interest.

Major George S. Merrill, of Lawrence, expresses his ideas of Pigeon Cove thus: "Perhaps in no spot along the coast has nature been so lavish of her beauties as at Pigeon Cove; the wildest rocky headlands confront the incoming waves from the Atlantic, while stretches of silvery beach glimmer between the crags, and a bit inland is a mighty forest through which paths have been cleared for such distances that one may wander from the busy village of summer saunterers into absolutely unbroken solitude."

Another very attractive place is Pigeon Hill. A visit to this eminence will be repaid by one of the most charming of views. Some very pretty homes are along the base of this hill, on the way to Rockport; among them are the Eames mansion; Elmwood, the residence of Mr. A. Goodwin's family; Uppercliff, the beautiful home of Mr. C. H. Cleaves and family; and Spring Cottage, a most charming place owned and occupied by Mr. Jason L. Curtis and family. Eglantine Lawn is another charming place by the seaside, the residence of Mr. Alonzo Tuttle. Many of these residences are occupied the entire year.

Another place of note is the stone bridge over the main road. Here one may stop to take a look down into the great granite quarries that can be seen from here, and wonder at the amount of stone that must have been quarried from the great pits.

The next attractive place ere we reach Rockport

is the picturesque Knowlton estate, with its fine old homestead and beautiful fields and mountains.

Thus Pigeon Cove has furnished summer tourists with a restful and healthful retreat, where ocean views, seaside rambles, good air from the balsamic pines, all produce for them pure enjoyment.

There are many charming woodland walks in this vicinity which afford great pleasure to the summer visitors, who turning directly from the view of old ocean, can in a short time be entirely out of sight of water among the tangled paths of the grand old woods. Pigeon Cove attracts a fine class of visitors, and abounds in many attractions which render it a most desirable place to pass the heated term.

The drive around the Cape continues through the town of Rockport, once a suburb of Gloucester, but in the year 1840 it was set off as a separate township. This town is appropriately named, and although large quantities of the quarried granite have been carried from here, great ledges are still to be seen everywhere. The constant quarrying of the granite has left deep ravines and abysses open to view.

Rockport has a pretty beach, which is utilized as a drying place for the sea moss, which the gatherers of this aquatic plant use every season, and which beach is passed on this drive. When the sea moss is arranged in various places on the beach and raked out over the smooth white surface of the sand, the varied colorings of the moss are most charming to examine. This moss is gathered and sold to sea moss dealers, and makes a most delicious and nutritious blanc mange.

Rockport was once a mill city, as will be seen by the ruins of the cotton mill, which are also passed on this drive, but possibly its greatest notoriety has been gained by its great quarries and its beautiful summer resort, Land's End.

After passing the beach we continue along the business portion of Main street, turning into Mt. Pleasant street, and driving until we reach Land's End, one of the outermost points of the Cape, which abounds in historic lore and grand scenery, and at which point that fine hostelry, Turk's Head Inn, and the many fine cottages of its summer residents are situated; while just off the shore is Thacher's Island with its twin lighthouses.

Turk's Head Inn preserves in its name the historic story of Capt. John Smith of Pocahontas fame, who when sailing on a voyage of discovery about the year 1612, named the three islands off the outermost point of Cape Ann the Three Turks' Heads, in remembrance of the three Turks he decapitated, single-handed, in a combat at Constantinople.

The Inn's broad piazzas, so cool and inviting, give fine views of forest and ocean, and the winding avenues are adorned with elegant homes of the summer tourist.

The Inn gained a good portion of its popularity

OLD TREE, ROCKPORT ROAD.

when under the stewardship of Mr. A. A. Pocock, formerly steward of the Algonquin Club of Boston.

Leaving Land's End we return by the same route we came, pass through the streets of the town again, and turning into Main street are soon leaving Rockport behind, and descending Great Hill pass Beaver Dam Farm and note the stone structure on the farm land bearing the inscription. "Beaver Dam Farm, 1832." Cape Pond and its fine picnic grove are soon passed, and the tree growing out of a rock (of which an illustration is given), the picturesque residence of the late Hon. John J. Babson, Gloucester's historian, also the fine residence of Hon. B. F. Cook, unsurpassed views of the Bass Rocks settlement and beautiful views of farm land are among the points of interest we should see when driving through the "Farms."

After passing the Hildreth school house we turn to the right and continue along Main street, and Western avenue, till we reach our starting point, the Surfside, having enjoyed a ride of continual change of scenery and marked beauty.

Drive to Manchester.

HAVING basked in the rays of Magnolia's natural charms and cultivated elegance, although but a brief description will be given here, be prepared, when you take this drive, to view a still more fashionable and highly popular summer resort some three miles beyond Magnolia, bearing the old English name, Manchester.

This town celebrated its 250th anniversary in 1895, and doubtless in consequence of that occurrence much of its early history has become familiar to almost every one, as so much was written regarding the event, and the celebration was so largely attended by the resident tourists and people from all the surrounding cities.

But its importance and popularity as a summer resort are the topics of interest. Manchester has been the summer home particularly of wealthy Bostonians for the past fifty years, and as it grew into prominence tourists from all parts of the country succumbed to its attractions. Thus it has naturally made rapid strides in valuation, and popularity as a fashionable summer resort. In fact, the demand for property at Manchester the past few years has been so great that at times it was practically impossible to rent any good houses with a view of the sea, and a number of people gave up going there for the season. There is a great demand for land, and very few lots for sale. The success of the Essex County Club, together with low taxes, largely explains the increasing popularity of Manchester.

Before reaching the town, the intervening road between Magnolia and Manchester is a forest road of stately trees and tall densely growing shrubbery, and when riding beneath this primeval growth one experiences a sensation most delightful.

The town of Manchester has a most pleasant and advantageous position, being situated on the north shore of Massachusetts bay. It is but twenty-four miles from Boston, nine from Salem and seven from Gloucester. Essex and Hamilton are to the north of it, Beverly and Hamilton to the west. Thus so centrally located, the drives it affords the tourist are of a most enjoyable nature.

Manchester's coast line is remarkable for its rugged appearance, and together with its forest covered valleys, it has afforded picturesque sites for the costly residences which have been erected, enhanced still more by the finely laid out grounds on which the taste and skill of the landscape gardener have been put forth.

Here is the famous "Singing Beach," so named because at times the washing of the sea as it creeps over the sandy shore sends forth a musical sound that at once strikes the listener as peculiar. From this beach is seen the waters of Massachusetts bay, which present ever changing marine views.

Here, also, is the famous Masconomo House, one of the finest on the North Shore, preserving in its name the Indian legendry of Manchester. This hotel at once brings to mind the noted actress, Agnes Booth Schoeffel, to whom this hotel became an inheritance from her late noted husband, and where she spends her summers, together with the large number of celebrities in all the professional circles of life, and to whom this famous hotel has catered for years.

Here also is the cottage of the noted veteran actor, Joseph Proctor, which rests half way up the hill above the railroad track.

If you are a devotee to golf, tennis or yachting, your desire to visit Manchester will be aroused at once, for here are the Essex County Club's famous golf links and tennis courts and the Manchester Yacht Club's house.

A word in regard to the Essex County Club. It has gained great prominence in the world of sports, as the turf at its golf links is reputed to be the best on this side of the water. Mr. Joseph Lloyd, their golf instructor, is the well known winner of the championship at Chicago. Mr. J. M. Mackerell is his assistant. The tennis tournaments of the Club, their dinner parties and balls are of the "swellest" type, and thus the "smart" set from all the neighboring resorts all flock to Manchester and revel in this Club's social generosity.

The Manchester Yacht Club has as good a situation as any yacht club in the country, and as fine a membership—some 215 or more members, the cream of the North Shore. Some of the Corinthian and Eastern Yacht Clubs are among its members, and as the harbor commissioners gave the Club permission to anchor floats in front of their club house, and have dredged and straightened the channel, these are two important factors in its favor. Regattas are held every season, and the social functions at this Doric club house, with its elegant furnishings, are of the most *fin de siecle* type, and have a tendency to outrival the Essex County Club.

Among the other objects of interest in the town is the fine Memorial Building and Library erected and donated to the town by T. Jefferson Coolidge, Esq. The building is located on Union street near the center of the town, and is constructed of cut Ashler granite with seam faces—that is, the stone was taken from the quarries where it joined the occasional seams found in the ledge—the stone being of a handsome red color. The eastern end of the building is occupied by the town library, and the western end by the local Post of the Grand Army. Dividing the two sections is a sort of open partition of old English oak inlaid with genuine ancient carvings brought from across the water and centuries old. The Memorial Hall contains two bronze tablets to the memory of the soldiers and sailors of the town.

One of the handsomest residences here is that of U. S. Senator James McMillan, of Detroit. It is called "Eagle Head," an estate of 78 acres, and valued at $200,000. The property, besides bordering on the ocean, has a long frontage on the Gloucester and Beverly road, and is adjacent to the grounds of the Essex County Club.

Among the other residences which attract the attention of visitors are the picturesque buildings on Norton's Head, erected by the venerable Rev. Dr. Bartol, of Boston, including the River house, the Fort house, the Barn house, and others of quaint and fantastic shapes.

On Gale's Point is one of the prettiest drives in the town. Among the notable summer residences in this section are those of Gen. A. P. Rockwell, George D. Howe, F. M. Stanwood, Richard Stone, George M. Black, J. Warren Merrill, the J. L. Bremer estate, G. A. Putnam and Charles A. Reed.

Other prominent summer places are those of Russell Sturgis, Judge Ricker of Denver, C. E. Cotting and John A. Burnham, and the Grews, Wigglesworths and Dodges near Eagle Head, T. Jefferson Coolidge and Ernest Longfellow at Coolidge Point, and the Boardman estate, and Henry L. Higginson, the well-known Boston banker, at West Manchester.

Here also is a chapel erected by the Unitarians of the summer colony, and in which they take great pride, the sister of President Elliott of Harvard College being one of the trustees. A convenient Episcopal chapel is also erected near the Masconomo House.

If you delight to view beautiful scenery, summer homes equally as beautiful, fine equipages, and all else that signifies immense wealth, great culture and "smart" social life, drive to Manchester and you will find it there.

The drive from Gloucester is both picturesque and delightful, along Western avenue, passing Magnolia and riding directly on. A view of the ocean may be obtained a greater part of the way, and the ride is replete with pleasure.

Around the "Big Heater."

ANOTHER very popular drive is that known as around the "Big Heater." You start along Western avenue, turning into Essex avenue and pass through West Gloucester, continuing on until you reach Essex, when you turn to the left and find a delightful drive through the woods a great portion of the distance—the very quintessence of country scenery. You arrive at Manchester, and the contrast presented on the drive to Gloucester, which gives such fine sea views, spoken of in the drive to Manchester, renders it an outing long to be remembered with pleasure. The distance is some seventeen miles, and the drive should be taken leisurely in order to be fully enjoyed.

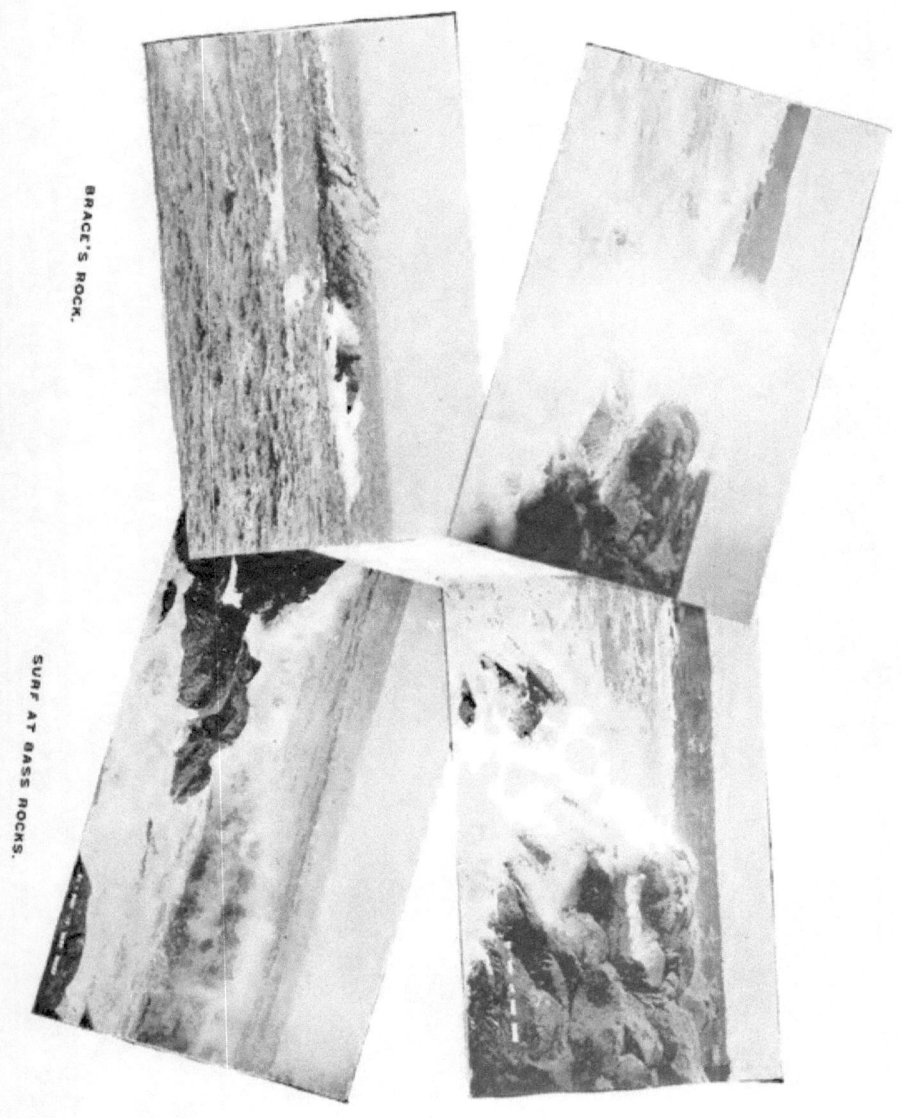

BRACE'S ROCK.

SURF AT BASS ROCKS.

The Old Rockport Road.

IN addition to the drives which have been mentioned, Gloucester abounds in most delightful walks, where the lover of nature can revel in the beauties so lavishly bestowed. Among these walks is one which teems with most beautiful scenery and affords much pleasure. It is known as the Old Rockport Road.

In the days agone it was the travelled highway between Gloucester and Rockport, and is entered from the city proper by passing up Maplewood avenue near its junction with Poplar street, on the right hand side after passing the Gloucester Net and Twine Company's buildings. It can also be reached on Washington street by passing through Derby, Grove or Poplar streets into Maplewood avenue. The road was at one time passable for vehicles, but it has been out of repair so long that there is not much comfort with a vehicle, but it is very good for horseback riding.

You pass along, oftentimes pausing to get glimpses of the fine scenery of the city on one hand and the grand old forests on the other. It carries with it also a view of the famed Dogtown, to which allusion is made in another chapter. The road winds in and out in a serpentine fashion, now ascending to a sightly elevation then descending into the valley. Now and then you pass an old cellar betokening that some family lived their lives here and experienced the joys and sorrows pertaining to the earthly existence, but now all is solitude and nature fully asserts her sway.

After sauntering a mile or more, you will observe to the right a high elevation known as Railcut hill, which is the second highest land in the city, coming next to Thompson's Mountain, West Gloucester. It will be known by the tripod erected thereon by the triangulation survey and forms a prominent landmark. Here a magnificent ocean view is obtained which will well repay one for the walk, and you enjoy one of the grandest outlooks which is afforded in Gloucester's fair borders.

After feasting the eye on the maritime view and inhaling the cool breeze, the walk can be resumed at leisure, stopping occasionally to pick some of the luscious berries, if it is the berry season, and in due time you will reach the main Rockport road, where you can board the electrics and enjoy the homeward ride through the Farms, taking in Little Good Harbor Beach, Bass Rocks and the beautiful maritime panorama which this section affords.

Drive to Dogtown.

AS the present age teems with interest in all that concerns the days of the Revolutionary War, and prominent people, with equally prominent ancestry, deem it an honor to swell the membership of the societies bearing the names of "Sons of the Revolution" and "Colonial Dames"; and as human nature finds no greater impetus for the awakening of the weird, fanciful and speculative characteristics of their compositions than when viewing a deserted village, a fast decaying ancient house, a ruined castle or a lonely spot, therefore do not forget to visit Gloucester's "Deserted Village" of Revolutionary fame bearing the peculiar name of "Dogtown." There are various routes by which it can be reached, both for the convenience of the pedestrian and those bent on a pleasure drive.

One of the recent local publications is a little volume entitled "In the Heart of Cape Ann, or the Story of Dogtown," by Charles E. Mann, finely illustrated by Catherine M. Follansbee. This little book gives descriptions of the famous characters of Dogtown, a map with the cellars and houses indicated and the routes by which they can be reached, and for a thorough knowledge of Dogtown this volume will be indispensable. The price is but 50 cents, and it may be found at the bookstores. Some of the approaches to Dogtown enumerated will not be amiss here.

Driving up Washington street past the railroad station, we soon reach the old historic Ellery house and "Meeting House Green," with Poplar street on the right hand side, into which we turn, then into Cherry street and into Dogtown. By Mann's map you have indicated all the cellars and sites of the houses of the famous settlers and witches of Dogtown, which are significant of the sorrow the Revolution brought to this settlement.

Another route is as follows: If you are in Riverdale near Goose Cove, turn into the road at the Cove, pass Dr. Wetherell's villa, where soon can be seen that curious rock, the "Whale's Jaw." This is a very pretty drive, and you descend Pilgrim Hill to the main road, which you pursue, turning to the left, and soon reach Stanwood street, which also leads past many of these famous cellars.

But why is this deserted village called Dogtown, I hear you query. Tradition says that when the call for enlistment in the army and navy of the Revolution came, our sturdy ancestors took up arms and bidding their brave wives farewell, departed for the scene of battle, many of them nevermore to return.

Then the widows each procured a dog as their

future protectors, and that gave rise to the name, and the herbs and berries which they gathered on these lone hills were carried to market and yielded them their daily bread.

Thus the ancient cellars, grass-grown roads and the weird traditions of the witches who lived there, still impart to the observer an intense melancholy interest in this deserted hamlet, and as you wander over Dogtown you will fully realize with the poet,—

> "Now the sounds of population fail;
> No cheerful murmurs fluctuate the gale;
> No busy steps the grass-grown foot way tread;
> But all the flowing flush of life is fled."

A Day's Outing on Annisquam River.

ONE of the most charming experiences to be enjoyed on Cape Ann is an outing on Annisquam river. You start from the outer harbor with the tide at half flood, in a comfortable row-boat or steam launch, having some one with you who is familiar with the river.

Entering the canal which connects the outer harbor with the river, you pass along by the well known "Donefudging" landing, with the brick almshouse and farm on the right, then under the railroad bridge, and the busy scene of the Cape Ann Anchor Works, Drop Forge Company's Works and Cape Ann Shoe Company's manufactory looms up on the river's bank. Keeping along on the bosom of the river, Wolf Hill attracts our attention, and the gardens and dwellings of ward six present a pleasing appearance.

As we are out for the day we will not hurry, but take our time, and instead of keeping down river, we steer our boat into Little river and navigate that beautiful stream. Russ' island forms the right bank going up, and the summer residences—Biskie Head, belonging to W. J. Maddocks; Riverside, the cozy cottage of George Steele—form attractive pictures; we then pass on up to the head of the river at West Gloucester, passing Stanwood's Point and Fernwood on the left with their colonies of summer residents, and Presson's Point on the right, both of which are alluded to more fully in the "Drive Around West Gloucester." You keep along to the extreme limit, which carries you to the harbor on Essex avenue, then retrace your way, entering Annisquam river opposite Wolf Hill.

Wolf Hill is a magnificent spot for a summer's sojourn, it being high and airy, with exquisite views of river and bay, with all the comforts of a summer residence, and only ten minutes ride to the post office and within seven minutes walk of the electrics, which pass the head of Marsh street every half hour.

A spot of clean white sand lies right off Wolf Hill, comprising several acres. This is the grand bathing place. It is easily accessible, and at half tide or low tide can be utilized, and forms a great attraction. Large numbers of summer residents avail themselves of this great privilege. There are also splendid bathing facilities in the cove next to Hodgkins' landing.

Among those having residences here are Messrs. Thaddeus E. Friend, Charles A. Mason, George H. Procter, Henry Center, Melvin Haskell, Charles C. Boardman, Isaac A. Smith, Charles H. Boynton, Frank H. Shute, Loring B. Haskell, Bennett Griffin,

Frank O. Griffin, Howard Haskell, Edward S. Griffin, Walter L. Rowe, David O. Frost, Fitz J. Babson, Simeon A. Burnham, Mrs. Lucy E. Friend (Glenmere), and Mrs. Addison Center of Melrose.

The next elevation, separated by a little cove, is a most charming spot. Nestling at the base is Shiloh Lodge, for many years the summer resort of the lamented George W. Smith and family, of Boston, whose annual coming rendered it extremely pleasant for the many friends who were here entertained in a most royal manner. Mr. Smith was among the first to find out the beauties and comforts of Annisquam river as a summer resort, and he built a house on Russ' Island, which was destroyed by fire, afterwards removing to this spot. The cottage has been greatly enlarged and improved, and is now owned by Dr. F. W. A. Bergengren of Lynn. Other cottages in the vicinity are those of Mrs. Charles H. Hildreth, Messrs. Calvin F. Hopkins, Fitz E. Oakes, William H. Dennen, Sidney S. Sylvester, and Frank Whittemore of Cambridge. Next on the same side is the famous Montezuma Camp, owned by Mr. Frank Stanwood.

Then crossing over to Russ' Island is the cottage of Mr. James Pettigrew, also the Spring and Wharf cottages, and those of Messrs. Buckingham and Chamberlain. The little island next appearing is in a cozy position, and is occupied by Mr. Richard Perkins.

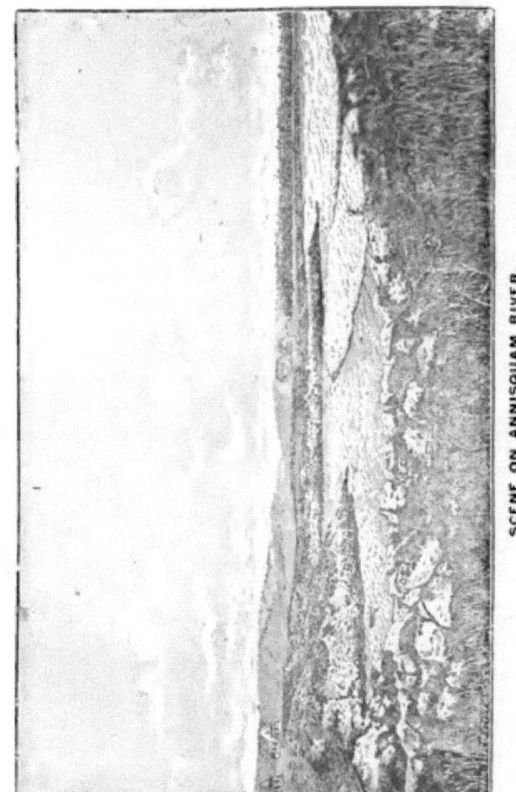
SCENE ON ANNISQUAM RIVER.

Then you draw near to Merchant's Island, formerly Pearce's, owned by Mr. Simeon Merchant, familiarly known as "Uncle Simeon." Here is a fine picnic grove which is brought into frequent use during the summer months. There are some twenty-five cottages on the island, which are let each season to families from the city proper, Charlestown, Chelsea and contiguous cities, and solid comfort is taken at this well known retreat. There is fun galore, and those who pass one season there are anxious to go again.

Opposite the island and midway of the river is a sand-spit an eighth of a mile in length, which at low tide forms one of the finest bathing places imaginable, being perfectly safe and the water pure and invigorating.

The scene from this point is charming in the extreme. Across the river at Brown's landing is a settlement of cottages known as Rocky Point, and a little farther along is Thurston's Point with its settlement. Here let us come to anchor right off the stone wharf. Of course you have brought your fishing-lines, frying-pan and boiler, and if you have no bait it will not take long to dig a few clams. This is a famous place for salt water perch, better known as cunners, and in a short time you will have all you want to cook. Then some of the men of the party will start a fire, while others have secured some toothsome clams, and fried perch, boiled clams, or perhaps a clam chowder, will add to the mid-day meal and appease that prodigious appetite which this outing has stimulated.

After dinner you can keep on down the river, passing Jones' creek on the left and Wheeler's Point on the right. This Point has attained a well deserved popularity as a charming spot to pass the summer months, being most advantageously situated and commanding a view which is unsurpassed for beautiful effects. Camp Coot occupies a position close to the water, and its occupants enjoy the delights of camp life during the season.

Turning sharp to the right you enter Mill creek, and it will well repay you to turn the bow of your boat up this stream and follow it to its source. To the left as you enter the creek, is Riggs' Point, and the remnants of the old wharf where Samuel Riggs carried on the fishing business previous to the Revolutionary War (and it was carried on there before his time, as he did not build the wharf or warehouses which heretofore existed; he built only the drying-houses that stood further back on the hill, and which were torn down some sixty years ago). All about here was the scene of much activity in the old-time fisheries. A remnant of an old wharf is visible at Wheeler's Point, also at Goose Cove.

The passage up the creek is replete with pleasure, with Wheeler's Point on the right and Riverdale on the left. At half tide you can row up to the old mill,

CAMBRIDGE COLONY, ANNISQUAM.

and if you choose can make a landing and examine the soldiers' monument, and then retrace your way to the main river. The numerous clam houses on the banks of the creek, and the piles of white shells visible, speak well of the industry of the people; and most of the houses in the village have been paid for out of the discounts from the clam banks. The land hereabouts is mostly used for summer outings, and it is admirably adapted for the purpose.

Once more into the main river, you get a view of Annisquam Point, also the clean white beach—the beginning of the far-famed Wingaersheek beach—the bridge over Annisquam river and Lobster Cove. If you have the time to spare and the tide serves, go up the cove, the head of which is very near the Universalist church, and it will prove a very interesting detour.

On your return, or if you conclude to keep on in the cove, you have a view of the Cambridge Settlement with its attractive dwellings and the well kept lawns, the summer house of George J. Marsh, and soon Annisquam lighthouse and Ipswich bay open up with all their summer loveliness. Cross over and take in the beauties of Wingaersheek beach, and the fine stone houses on the "Loaf" owned by Edwin C. Hawkes, Esq., of Buffalo, N. Y. What a stretch of clean white sand! What opportunities for boating, bathing and the like! What a picture of beauty on a summer afternoon! And it does not take much stretch of imagination to look forward to a few years in the future when a summer hotel will grace some of the attractive knolls, and a gay company will sport and draw strength and inspiration from nature's well filled storehouse.

Now having made the tour of the river and bay, the home journey is taken up river. You can vary this, if you choose, by entering Jones' Creek on your right, and take the passage around the island. With the tide in your favor, you slip easily along and reach the stone pier. Then you keep on until you come to the creek, which will carry you out near Russ' island, making a grand detour of the river which is filled with many surprises. Continuing the way over the route which you came, you are soon at the canal and into Gloucester harbor again, having enjoyed one of the most pleasurable trips to be found on the coast of New England, a repetition of which will afford new pleasures and delights.

This river forms the connecting link between Gloucester harbor and Ipswich bay, and its beauties are thoroughly appreciated by hundreds of tourists who take this route to avoid the much longer one that necessitates going around the Cape.

E. C. HAWKES' RESIDENCE, WINGAERSHEEK BEACH.

The Nashua Settlement and Revere Street.

IN the drive around the Cape there are two detours which might be made. Just to the rear of the Universalist church at Annisquam is Nashua street, which leads to the Nashua Settlement, where many summer cottages are situated. It will be found a very pleasant point to visit, offering a fine view of Ipswich bay and its pleasant surroundings.

Returning to the main road, we drive a short distance to the eastward and enter Revere street, which extends about one mile into the woods, making a very pleasant summer drive. The street leads up to the house now owned and occupied by Mr. David Dennison. The house is one hundred and sixty-nine years old, and was built by Mr. George Dennison, the first settler. Persons visiting the Dennison place should not neglect to get a drink of water from the celebrated spring, which they will find to be cool and sparkling, and the best on the Cape.

On the drive over this street you can obtain a good view of the Rockport Granite Company's quarries, and the "Blondin," used for hoisting and handling blocks of granite from the quarry. A fine view of Ipswich bay also meets the eye.

West Gloucester Again.

[After the chapter entitled "Around the Parish" had been printed, a friend living in that vicinity called our attention to the "Dark Hole Road" so called, and other pleasant spots in West Gloucester, to which we had not alluded. We therefore determined to devote another chapter to West Gloucester, and we give it here.—Pubs.]

THE hand of art and of improvement has not wholly changed all of the old roads and rustic by-ways in the village of West Gloucester. A few still remain picturesque and attractive by their crookedness, their narrowness, winding along under the shade of primeval trees, through whose wide-spreading branches one often looks with delight upon rare bits of scenery.

The "Dark Hole Road," better adapted now for pedestrian travel than as a carriage road, is beautiful and attractive from the very neglect to which it has been left. Entrance to this road is almost directly opposite the Congregational church, and it winds along for a distance of about a mile, when the traveller comes out into the open country on "Turtle Pond Hill" "at the parting of the ways."

The road to the right leads "'round the parish," coming out on Concord street; the road to the left leads down the hill to the cemetery and to the parting of the roads again. Follow the road to the right till you come to the bridge over the river, cross the bridge, walk or drive on through a lovely region of country till the road to Conomo Point is reached. Here again the traveller hesitates and questions whether to go on a short distance, where two roads will again confront him, the road to the left leading through one of the most beautiful bits of forest roads in Essex county, coming out to Essex avenue near the guide-board, which points you east to Gloucester and west to Essex, Hamilton and Ipswich. The road to the right leads on past the well cultivated farm of Mr. Alvah Lufkin, through a most charming circuitous narrow roadway, bounded on either side by old stone walls covered with grey moss and many colored lichens, while the air is fragant with barberry blossoms, sweet briers, wild roses, viburnums, golden rod, the hemlock and pines.

Along this delightful old road which leads past the " island school house " to the causeway across the marshes to the town of Essex, the perspective views of the ocean and the river are exquisite, while in the foreground the broad marshes with their emerald tints in early spring, changing into golden brown in the early autumn, make a picture from which the eye never turns with weariness.

The drive " Around the Parish " is a favorite one. Riding from Gloucester over Essex avenue, leave the avenue at Concord street, and after a drive under the shade of maples, pines, white birches, and along a pretty stretch of willows, where the wild grape vine grows luxuriantly, twining its multitude of tendrils and dark glossy leaves over the stone walls and high among the branches of trees and shrubs, and the air is filled with delicious perfumes of wild roses, elder blooms and pines, you reach the end of this route just above the old Haskell saw-mill, and you have seen "many objects in their Arcadian simplicity."

Drive on a few rods, turn down by the mill into the narrow shady road, bordered on one side by marshes and cultivated fields, on the other by stone walls, trees and a variety of shrubs and flowers. This road brings you to the pleasant summer residence of Mr. John J. Pew; turn to the left, and a little farther on you come to the home of Mr. Thomas Haskell. The old house where he spent the first years of his married life is still standing, while just a few rods distant is the more modern house he had built not many years previous to his death. Almost within speaking distance, along a well worn foot-path, through the old gateway, is the low old-fashioned vine-covered cottage where Mr. Haskell's sister lived, and familiarly known all about "the parish" as "Aunt Hitty." These two people are historic characters, and their names are written beside Wendell Phillips, Lucy Stone and the long list of slavery, non-resistance and temperance reformers, who have passed on to the higher life.

Returning from the cottage, go through the farmyard to the beautiful pine grove, beneath the generous shade of which winds a charming wooded road; follow on till you come to the gate, which one finds easy to open, then out again into the open highway, where three roads confront the traveller. The one to the right takes you between hedge rows of blueberry and barberry bushes, out over the bridge near the Haskell school house, and here again one can follow his own choice. Go to the left, " 'round the parish," or follow the straight road out onto Essex avenue. Drive to the left to Essex, or make another divergence to the left, and you come again onto Essex avenue. The third, or middle road, leads to Conomo Point.

The summer tourist or whoever may chance to journey for pleasure along these old roads will find much to delight the eye as they pass on "through pleasant valleys, under the brows of hills, along by the winding river, now half way up some gentle eminence that commands charming views of the village, or winding round a hill and giving us a new view of the scenes we have just passed."

Mount Anne, or Tompson's Mountain.

MOUNT ANNE is the highest point of land on Cape Ann, and proves a very attractive feature, and is annually visited by a large number of delighted tourists. This has been briefly alluded to in the drive "Around the Parish," but is deserving of further mention.

The mountain is easy of access by two roads, the first near Liberty Hall, and the other, farther on, leading to the left from the old Haskell saw-mill through what is known as "Queechy Run" road. Both of these roads are attractive, leading on beside a winding brook, bordered on either side with ferns and the early spring flowers, and in the autumn the brilliant cardinal flowers mirror themselves in its brown depths. This shady pathway leads to the very summit of the mountain, where one looks out upon magnificent views of both inland and ocean scenery.

Not far from "Queechy Run" road is "Braewood," the home of Miss Maria H. Bray, whose house during the summer season is the resort for pleasant people, who find a charm and attraction in the social life of this home. There is also a fascination in this quiet retreat, from the large area of pine woods which surrounds it and intercepts to a certain extent the full force and harshness of the sea air, leaving just enough of the salt oxygen to mingle with the tonic of the pines and hemlocks, thus forming an invigorating atmosphere. It is a peaceful summer resort for the weary and those who want rest and pleasant home life.

Old Meeting House Hill.

TURNING to the left from Concord street less than a mile from Essex avenue, is Tompson street, still known by its local name of "Old Meeting House Road." After leaving the dwellings at the junction of Concord and Tompson streets not a building is to be seen in the whole distance to the crossing of Bray street, perhaps a mile and a half away.

Tompson street leads first up a steep hill from which a beautiful view can be obtained of Annisquam river and the Harbor village, the islands and Riverdale shore, with pleasant homes and gardens on the West Gloucester side in the immediate foreground, a little farther to the right "frost flung" walls and scattering foundation stones mark the "old Bray place," the boundaries of the garden about the old cellar being well defined, with here and there shoots of old orchard trees.

The road winds along into a valley where on the left a mowing field shows where once was "Avery's orchard." Farther along we are told stood the old house, from which Samuel Avery and his brother John, the last males of their name in the second parish, went out the day that the waves closed over them near the beach of Wingaersheek.

Along through a way bordered with alders and birches and bright with wild flowers, a turn up another hill and on your right is the foundations of an old tavern, so it is said, although who was its tenant the traditions do not say, then a little farther and you are on "Old Meeting House Hill," the only trace of the old church being a few scattering stones of its foundation, there for nearly seven score years stood the old house of worship, torn down in 1846. The hill is an elevation with a fine view from its summit.

In front of the church was the ground used for military evolutions in the "training days" of our ancestors. Farther to the west Bray street crosses, and until a few year ago an ancient house stood near which was the residence of the first pastor of the Parish, Rev. Samuel Tompson, mentioned in another chapter. From Bray street Tompson continues northwester until passing the "old burying ground," it comes out upon Concord street again.

NANNIE C. BOHLIN

An Up-to-Date Gloucester Fishing Vessel.

A MODERN type of fishing vessel is the pride and delight of every true Gloucesterite, and the ownership or command of one is the hope of every brawny fisherman who expects some day to prefix "Skipper" to his name. Well may the sons of Gloucester feel proud; and pardonable the pride of every man who commands one of the marine architect's skill.

A Gloucester skipper considers his staunch vessel his ocean home. Firmly and deeply attached to her, he knows thoroughly her every good quality and unflinchingly lauds her worthiness in many an interesting argument with his brother commanders.

And he is proud of the looks of his pet, too, and pays as much attention to her outward appearance as to her inward comfort. Many times a year she is hauled out on the marine railways and treated to handsome coats of paint. Spars are kept bright, decks clean, and a general air of neatness made to pervade the whole craft.

The accompanying cut is a fine representation of a model modern fishing schooner. Note her handsome sheer, perfect fitting sails, long bowsprit and trim rig. Is she not every whit as handsome as the proud yachts which flit about like butterflies on the summer seas?

Remember, dear reader, that these modern fishing craft are of no "rule of thumb" origin. They are drafted, moulded and modelled with the greatest care by architects of rank like Capt. G. Melvin McClain, Stewart and Binney and others of note. Even the lamented Burgess and Lawlor took pride in designing fishing craft.

Their speed, power, stability and carrying capacity then are not to be wondered at when it is remembered how they are designed, added to the fact that they are built in the strongest possible manner. Don't be surprised if you should chance to be enjoying a yachting cruise along shore some summer, and one of these white-winged fishing craft should come up under your lee, cross your bow and go off to windward about her business. Many like instances have happened and do occur every season.

It would require more space than can be afforded here to tell the stories of some of these crafts, of their wonderful sailing qualities; their ability to carry sail; the terrible weather they will face, "beating" up Boston bay in the winter time; and entering Boston harbor when steamers would not dare leave port. All these must be made tales by themselves.

[The cuts of vessels used in this volume to represent up-to-date fishing crafts are taken from among the fleet owned by Mr. William H. Jordan of this city, who conducts one of the leading concerns of this port.]

CITY HALL.

GILBERT HOME.

HUNTRESS HOME.

HIGH SCHOOL.

The Surfside Hotel.

A FIRST-CLASS hotel is a great desideratum to a town or city, and such an one in every respect is the Surfside, under the management of Mr. F. H. Sawyer, who made a successful initiatory season in 1895.

The house was formerly known as the Pavilion, and occupies a commanding position on Pavilion Beach, within five minutes' walk of the post office.

It has a good harbor and ocean view, and everything is new and clean with good attendance. Excellent cuisine, nice table linen, and dining hall appointments unsurpassed. The sleeping accommodations are of a high order of excellence, luxuriant beds and modern furniture. Thoroughly screened. Perfect drainage.

Good bathing, boating, fishing and delightful woodland rides. It will be observed that many of the drives in this little volume start from the Surfside. This was on account of the choice central location. We feel assured reader that you will find a good home-like hotel at the Surfside.

Oldest Universalist Church in America. Procter Building—"Old Corner." City Hall.
Unitarian Church and Sawyer Library. High School.

Solid Facts Concerning Gloucester.

STARTING from Gloucester we have taken you, in these short articles, around the pleasant drives which extend through and from Cape Ann. We doubt whether in the variety which they afford their equal can be found anywhere along the coast—now skirting the pleasant shore bathed with the never ceasing flow and ebb of old ocean, and then in and through the shaded wood and country road. And the more you drive the more you come to love them for their sense of rest and quiet, and to long for them with each returning summer season. We know you will enjoy them all, you cannot help it.

Gloucester bids you welcome to her open hospitality. We bid you come again and again to her city streets and quiet lanes. We bid you drink deep of the health giving life which she so abundantly supplies. And before closing this small volume we give just a word about her and her history, so well written by one of her enthusiastic lovers who looks confidently into that future which must come to a place so well favored by nature and by fortune:

"Gloucester, in Essex county, is charmingly situated on Cape Ann, the most prominent point of land on the northeastern coast of Massachusetts. Its shores are washed by the waves of the broad Atlantic as well as those of Massachusetts bay. Its broad, capacious and beautiful harbor is one of the best along the whole seaboard.

Gloucester's settlement dates as early as 1623, but centuries before its shores were visited by the hardy Norsemen, and even in 1605 by the courageous adventurers who were then exploring the New World. It was incorporated as a town in 1642, and for two hundred and fifty years its history has been honorable and full of brave deeds and tenacious activity. Its population (1896) is 29,000.

Situated on a branch of the Boston and Maine railroad, thirty-two miles from Boston, Gloucester has the advantage of splendid train service, both local and express, with low transportation rates. It is the centre of an electric railroad system, which is admirably equipped and furnishes easy connection with all parts of the Cape and Essex county.

As a fishing port it is the largest in the United States; it is the head centre of the fresh and salt fish industry. It has first-class steamer service for freight and passengers. Its harbor is safe and easy of access. Its next largest industry is the granite, and this is constantly growing in extent and value. It has a large foreign import trade in salt, and domestic trade in lumber and coal. The leading industries are ship-building, fish glue, anchors, oil clothing, net and twine, seines, boots and shoes. Its mail facilities are first-class. It has the best water system in Massachusetts, electric light and gas plants, schools of the highest grade, churches of all denominations, well-endowed public library, Memorial Hospital, Old People's Homes, a superior fire department, and, best of all, low valuation and moderate tax rate, with low municipal debt.

Unusual facilities are offered to manufacturers of all kinds, and it will pay any one desiring good location and good and cheap help to look Gloucester over. It has live merchant organizations in the shape of the Board of Trade and the energetic Business Men's Association, which numbers four hundred members and has splendidly equipped rooms in the very business centre of the city. Although a city of good size, it takes high rank as a sober, industrious, law-loving population.

As a summer resort its equal cannot be found along the North Shore, with the very best of hotels and boarding-houses. Delightful locations for owning one's own home. Beautiful drives along the shore, or into the country, over well-kept roads.

The merchants are hustlers, and in catering to retail trade they offer the finest stock of goods and the lowest prices. Strangers find hearty welcome to the city, and are soon made to feel at home. Look Gloucester over and watch its future. It is bound to grow and prosper."

Gloucester Harbor, 1830.

THE accompanying illustration is a representation of the outer harbor, taken from the beach at Western avenue in 1830. How different is the view at this day. All along the water front is built up, and the hill, which at that time was bare of dwelling houses, is now covered with some of the finest residences in the city.

The old windmill, which then occupied the position where the Surfside hotel now stands, was for many years an important landmark on entering the harbor. It was erected in 1814 by Mr. Ignatius Webber, a successful shipmaster, who retired from commercial pursuits in 1806, and for three years subsequently was connected with Messrs. Aaron and Henry Plumer in carrying on the ropewalk (which may be seen in the illustration), which was built by Capt. Webber and Mr. Aaron Plumer in 1803, and sold at auction about 1810 to Mr. John Somes, Jr., for $4550.

The windmill was removed to Commercial street when the Pavilion (now Surfside hotel) was erected, and was so badly injured by fire July 5, 1877, that it was sold and removed.

GLOUCESTER HARBOR, 1830.

The Old Fort and Gloucester Harbor in 1837.

THE annexed engraving gives a capital view of the old Fort and Gloucester harbor in 1837. What a great change has been effected since that time. Then there was but one building, besides the ruins, at the Fort, now it is covered with dwellings and storehouses, and is one of the busiest spots in the city. Its entire water front has been converted into fine wharves, forming one of the most valuable pieces of property hereabouts.

The Grand Banker and pinkey, typical crafts of those days, look as natural as can be. What a contrast to the up-to-date craft of to-day.

A drive around the old Fort is replete with interest, giving a fine harbor view. It is very easily reached from the western end of Main street, turning into Commercial street and at the end of Commercial street turning to the right or to the left.

THE OLD FORT AND GLOUCESTER HARBOR IN 1837.

HENRY M. STANLEY.

Errata.

On page 9 the schooner Rigel was engaged in the fletched halibut fishery, instead of the herring.

On page 33, it should read, Miss Martha Marvin, instead of "Marion," washed off the rocks at Rafe's Chasm.

[Copyright, 1890, by PROCTER BROTHERS.]

www.ingramcontent.com/pod-product-compliance
Lightning Source LLC
Chambersburg PA
CBHW030310170426
43202CB00009B/949